OBJECTIONS
TO
CHRISTIAN BELIEF

This is an age when the foundations of Christian belief are being called in question. The case against Christianity cannot be met by the mere repetition of old arguments nor by any slick "apologetic". The primary need is to understand as clearly and deeply as possible what the fundamental objections to Christian belief now are. The four lectures here published were delivered in Cambridge with a view to promoting an understanding of some of these objections. The authors are members of the Faculty of Divinity in the University, but they were addressing lay people in general, so that what they said should be of interest to a much wider audience than could be present at the lectures. Each lecture was subsequently discussed by many study groups in the University, and the book should be useful for both individual and group study elsewhere. For thoughtful people today, Christian faith can be reached or maintained only by way of an open-minded and painful reckoning with all that tells against it.

OBJECTIONS TO CHRISTIAN BELIEF

D. M. MACKINNON
H. A. WILLIAMS
A. R. VIDLER
J. S. BEZZANT

With an Introduction by
A. R. VIDLER

Constable · London

Published by CONSTABLE & CO LTD
10-12 Orange Street London WC2

First Published 1963

Made and printed in Great Britain by
The Garden City Press Limited
Letchworth, Hertfordshire

CONTENTS

CONTENTS

INTRODUCTION

THIS course of lectures was
given in Cambridge in February 1963 under the
auspices of the Divinity Faculty. But they were
open lectures, i.e. addressed to the University as a
whole, not to theological students. It is much to
be desired that representatives of the different
Faculties should take opportunities of speaking
to as large a public as possible, so overcoming the
academic tendency to a narrow specialization or
departmentalism.

The aim of the lectures, which are here published practically as they were delivered, was not
to provide answers to objections to Christian
belief. There is a spate of books which set out to do

that. We hold that it is more important to try to plumb the depths of the objections, without complacently assuming that answers are readily available. Above all in a university, Christians must seek to understand the fundamental doubts to which their faith is exposed in this age of the world. These lectures were intended to contribute to that kind of understanding. They were thus intended to be disturbing rather than reassuring. Belief in Christianity, or in anything else, if it is to be mature, must want to face the worst that can be said against it and to evade no difficulties. As W. H. Mallock said, "no one is fit to encounter an adversary's case successfully unless he can make it for the moment his own, unless he can put it more forcibly than the adversary could put it for himself, and take account not only of what the adversary says, but also of the best he *might say*, if only he had chanced to think of it".

It may be thought that objections to Christian belief would be more convincingly stated by unbelievers than by believers. Certainly Christians should listen attentively to all who submit their beliefs to an acute and sensitive criticism. But the objections are likely to be perceived and felt even more keenly by people who, maybe for many years, have been living with one foot in Christian belief and the other resolutely planted in the radical unbelief of the contemporary world, so that they are, as it were, torn between the two. If there is to be a profound recovery of

Christian belief—or a profound rejection of it—
it will surely come out of such an experience
rather than out of an awareness of only one side
of the question.

It has been said that "the problem of evil is
pregnant with mysteries. Perhaps it is more
important and shows more insight to be aware of
these mysteries, and even of the impossibility of
solving them, than to find consolation in an easy
and hence illusory logical issue out of this most
issueless and tragic of all problems" (E. Lampert).
There is not very much that is new in the problem
of evil, but as a result of advances in the sciences,
of a larger moral sensibility and of changes in the
philosophical climate there are today genuinely
new or greatly intensified challenges to Christian
belief. It is some of them that these lectures were
concerned to explore.

A. R. Vidler

King's College
Cambridge

MORAL
OBJECTIONS

D. M. MACKINNON

CHRISTIANITY is regularly
presented as a way of life and as such it is presented as demanding from those who profess it a
certain pattern of moral behaviour. From this
pattern Christians may depart; but with very
important differences between divergent traditions of Christian faith and practice (e.g. over
artificial contraception), there is a certain measure
of agreement concerning what constitutes Christian moral behaviour. Now it is one of the features
of the world in which we live that this venerable
tradition is under fire from a great many direc-
tions, and subject to critical pressures at a number
of different levels. It is with the characterization

of some of these criticisms that I am concerned tonight.

Thus there has been a great deal of discussion recently in the press and elsewhere arising out of Professor Carstairs' series of Reith Lectures. I am not concerned with the accuracy with which Professor Carstairs' own mind has been reported; what I want simply to advertise is that in these discussions the Christian tradition has been attacked on the ground that it stresses the importance of premarital abstinence from sexual relations and fails either to reckon with psychological tensions such abstinence may set up in individuals, or to present any sort of adequate *positive* image of human life.

I want to concentrate on the latter more general criticism; it is a good example of the extent to which Christian morality is regarded as a morality of obligation, even of command. Christians may protest against this interpretation of what they say. They may argue roughly as follows: "While some Christian denominations may identify the sanction or authority of this morality with the will of God, in fact the great tradition of Christian thought has found that authority to reside not in an arbitrary divine fiat or command but in the ways in which what we are morally bound to do provides the road to our own actualization as human beings; we rise to the full stature of our humanity, we become truly human by obedience to the dictates of the moral law. This is the broad high road to true health, individual and collective alike".

If we apply this interpretation to help our understanding of the issues raised in Carstairs' broadcasts, we find that those issues are partly transformed. The claim is now one that those who condemn premarital sexual intercourse are wrong in fact. Such behaviour is perilously likely to prove destructive of the integrity, even of the stability and peace of mind, of those who practise it. They are failing to reckon with their total nature as human beings; they are isolating sexual activity from human life as a whole; although they claim to acknowledge its importance, they are failing to reckon with the extent to which its pressures invade and shape human life as a whole. What are conventionally called illicit relationships provide the sort of soil in which self-deceit and masquerade can flourish, and men and women are consequently easily estranged from the substance of their being. Whatever we may think of this sort of argument (and I shall have more to say on this issue later) we must allow that this sort of emphasis considerably mitigates, if not altogether alters, the presentation of Christian morality as an ethic of sheer obligation. We are no longer forced to see ourselves as restrained by the arbitrary dictates of a God; we are rather encouraged to see ourselves as enticed by the way of obligation to tread the road of our proper humanity.

But two very serious questions arise here.

(a) How adequate is the image of the good life which is offered? It can hardly be denied that a widespread obsessional preoccupation with the alleged great evil of the remarriage of divorced persons creates the impression that the core and centre of Christian moral teaching is a particular interpretation of the indissolubility of marriage; on this view it is taken as putting an appalling stigma on these second unions, of which we have all met examples, and know to have been more abundantly justified by their fruits than the frequently tragic human distress they have replaced. It is impossible to escape the impression that, to certain sorts of clergy, the effective exclusion from sacramental communion of divorced persons who have remarried is the highest form of the Church's moral witness. The cynic might well be tempted to say that the heartless zeal frequently displayed in the bearing of this particular testimony, is a way in which ecclesiastics compensate for their unwillingness to engage with other besetting moral issues of our age, for instance the moral permissibility of nuclear weapons.

I mention this issue, speaking in deliberately harsh terms (although no harsher perhaps than the callousness of our moral bigots merits) because it seems to pin-point the question immediately raised by the moral tradition which I have expounded. How adequate to human life as men and women live it is this image of the good life?

Does it do justice to the heights and depths, to the pity and terror, of life as we know it? It is this question which is in fact one of those raised by the many who speak of Christianity as life-denying rather than life-affirming or life-enhancing; and it is with that criticism before all others that this lecture is concerned. But let there be no mistake at this point. If we seek to rebut the criticisms brought against our Christian image of the good life by saying that thus and thus runs the writ of the divine law, we are simply assuming the language of an ethic of obligation. You cannot have it both ways; either this way of living is commended because it is self-justifying or it is commanded because it is the will of God. To introduce appeal to the divine will is to find sanction for the manner of human life in the command of a transcendent lawgiver.

(b) Yet there is another question, related to the former but distinguishable from it. How far in *the last analysis* does the kind of ethic of which I am speaking escape the charge of legalism? The moral law is, it is argued, the law of our proper nature; it is the form of a truly human existence. It is presented to us as something which both commands and attracts us because we are the sort of beings that we are. The law of morality argues strongly against all that involves us in violation of what we suppose the form of our proper nature to be; as a matter of historical fact acknowledgment of its authority has made men ready to resist,

15

faithful unto death, the dictates of tyrants, and of those who claim in the name of a so-called common good, to override the most elementary human decencies. But still that way of life to which it is said we are drawn, is presented as something over against us which commands us. It does not simply attract by seeming to enlarge the horizons of our existence; it is life-restricting rather than life-enhancing.

We have to reckon, if we are honest, with a strongly anti-nomian element in Christianity as a historical phenomenon. It shows itself in the New Testament in Paul's bitter arguments with himself concerning the Jewish law; it is present also in the Gospel according to St Luke. Although traditional believers may find it scandalous, it has always been there in the background, as if at some level of their being Christians were deeply aware of the relativity of legal categories, even if they could not define the Christian way of behaviour without their aid. What is it, we may ask, in human life, to which the notion of law sometimes alone effectively does justice? What of positive import can be salvaged from so much that seems to lend itself to the distortion of a way of life into something that bears perilous resemblance to a life-denying legalism? I want to suggest to you, and this again is a central theme of my whole lecture, that in a very confused way the tradition of which I have spoken and which I have criticized is seeking to do justice to the

16

element of restraint, of respect, in human life,
complex as that life is.

What is the place of restraint in morality?
There is a place for restraint. Human relationships can be irreparably damaged by absence of
respect and by absence of attention to the total
situation in which an agent is involved. We are
familiar with such violations at the level of collective existence when individual rights and liberties
are mercilessly sacrificed to the dynamism of the
totalitarian state. But we encounter them also at
the more intimate levels of personal life. A man
seeks to renew himself by accepting, in middle
age, the advances of a woman much younger than
himself; he plunges into the affair boldly, even
enthusiastically; but soon, even very soon, the
zest with which he gives himself to his adventure
is overshadowed by the necessity of deviousness,
of deceit, of make-believe intended no doubt to
preserve the façade of his marriage, but itself a
fearful violation of the respect he owes his wife
and family. To speak in these terms is not to
assume the tone of a censorious moralist; there is
much in human life both healing and creative,
that would shock the compilers of manuals of
moral theology. But respect, and the kind of
restraint that is closely bound up with it, is part
of the very stuff of human life, and we neglect its
claims at our peril. Although respect and restraint
are not the whole of morality, human relations
can be irreparably damaged by their absence.

17

The problem raised so far in this lecture may well be that of finding a definition of the restraint element in morality and indicating its proper place. How indeed is restraint related to life? To these issues we shall return; but the time has now come to move to a rather different set of problems, admitting, you will be glad to be told, of less formidably abstract treatment than what has gone before.

So I come to the second group of questions which I wish to raise. So far nothing has been said explicitly concerning the theological foundations of Christian morality; I have not even mentioned the supposed primacy given to the so-called "theological virtues" of faith, hope and charity. Later I shall have something to say on the subject of charity; for the time being I wish to restrict myself to faith and hope, and in particular to faith.

While the notion of faith is highly complex, it cannot be denied that faith, as the Christian understands it, includes as part of itself assent to certain propositions concerning matters of fact, and belief that what these propositions assert is supremely significant for human life, indeed for man's total posture under the sun. That this is so cannot be denied by those who emphasize in ways currently fashionable that Christian faith is primarily trust in a person; for the character of the trust given to that person is determined by belief concerning what he did and whom he is.

(a) Jesus of Nazareth belongs to history. He has a place, however obscure its details may be, in the story of the last years of the Jewish state between thirty and forty years before final catastrophe overtook it. He was a teacher, who spoke to men and women who lived in that situation, whose attitudes to the choices and emergencies that pressed upon them in their personal and collective existence were very various. His originality as a teacher lies partly in the permanent insight which continually he mediated in what he said, speaking relevantly and intelligibly to the men and women whom he addressed, but repeatedly transcending their immediate situation and by any reckoning, enriching the moral understanding of those belonging to ages yet unknown.

But for Christian faith this teacher is also the one who, by what he did, affected decisively the ultimate destiny of every man and woman contemporary with him, born before him and born after him. Of the greatness of this claim I shall have something to say in a moment. What I want to emphasize immediately is that it stands or falls by the truth or falsity of certain statements relating to matters of historical fact. Thus we may agree that Jesus was brought to his death in consequence of the impact made by his teaching. What men decided to do to him had something to do with the things he said to them, for instance the radical challenge he issued to every sort of legalism, and entrenched ecclesiastical hypocrisy.

But the claims which Christians make for that which he endured demand that he shall have approached his sufferings in a particular way, not simply as a luckless victim of uncontrolled circumstance, but as someone, who even if he found that circumstance uncontrollable, yet freely accepted the fact. No one who is in earnest concerning the foundations of Christian belief can pretend that his belief would not be radically affected, if he became convinced that as a matter of historical fact Jesus had never prayed in the garden of Gethsemane that the hour might pass from him and then after agony of prayer freely accepted his Father's will. Whether or not he did so pray is a matter of historical fact to be settled by methods precisely akin to those which Roman historians use to determine whether or not Julius Caesar was aiming at Oriental despotism before his assassination, or English historians of the sixteenth century to determine the arcana of Elizabeth's relations to Mary Queen of Scots. Now Christians must realize that the crucial importance of this issue for their faith raises grave doubts in their critics' minds concerning the honesty with which they will approach it. So much is at stake that the Christian will accept as proving that what he wants to believe happened, actually happened, evidence which as an historian, passing judgment on the claims of other events to be classed as actual, he would never have accepted.

We have got to realize the seriousness with which men urge that faith encourages dishonesty. The importance that the Christian is encouraged by the very nature of his faith to attach to such events as those I have mentioned, tends to obscure the honesty of the judgment he passes concerning them and affects adversely his intellectual honesty in general. Christians give weight, and must give weight to belief that certain events have actually happened; how far does this make them prejudiced and narrow and unwilling to open their minds to uncertainties concerning particular strands of human history? This objection is a moral objection in that it urges that faith, as the Christian understands it, is incompatible with a proper intellectual objectivity.

(b) Further, suppose we do allow that the events to which I have referred actually happened, what are the consequences to the way in which a man or woman sees human life of bestowing upon them the sort of significance which Christians claim they have? We have to allow that the ways in which this significance is represented are relative to particular cultures, and more seriously to particular and restricted human interests and concerns. Think for a moment of the apparatus of images and concepts whereby the notion of atonement is conveyed. If we speak of Christ's death as a sacrifice which takes away the sin of the world, however much we may refine the concept of sacrifice that we

21

employ, we are still putting ourselves in bondage to it; what of the man to whom the whole idea of sacrifice is not so much strange and repulsive as restricted and restricting? There is so much more in human life known and unknown than the kind of theological conceptions whereby we seek to capture the nature of atonement, can hope to lay hold of. We live in an age that is at once one of unprecedented excitement and unprecedented fear; but the demand that we should try to catch its terror and its glory in this network of particular theological conceptions asks that we should mutilate our sense both of its promise and its terror.

Those of you who are unwise enough to read the church press, will be familiar with a recent episode in which certain members of this University, were made the targets of unbridled venom on the part of religious conservatives; the latter saw quite rightly that their own cosy acquiescence in conventional ways of thought was menaced by the facts to which the critics called attention. We are not concerned in this lecture with the Philistine anti-intellectualism of the *Church Times*; but we must be concerned with the underlying failure to measure up to the relativity of the Christian reality which it expresses. To return:

It would indeed be hard to underestimate the damage done to the Christian understanding of the moral life by the sort of impoverishment of our fundamental theological categories which I have illustrated. These categories have become dated and stereotyped; but their continued use has helped to fetter on Christian tradition some most dangerous falsehoods and half-truths concerning the way men and women should live. Moreover they have done so precisely by the way in which they have imposed upon the central figure of Christian aspiration and devotion (the crucified Lord) the stamp of their own narrowly ecclesiastical pedigree.

It would be easy to point here to the attitude towards penal institutions and reform as encouraged, perhaps unconsciously, by acceptance of a penal substitutionary conception of the atonement. We need not deny a partial validity to the retributive analysis of punishment in order to be outraged by the supposition that the vindictive insatiability of the divine justice demands that the vials of wrath be poured out upon the innocent in ways that suggest that de Maistre spoke less than the truth when he said that the fundamental realities of the world were crime and punishment; he had better have said they were the fundamental constituents of being itself. But the idiom of sacrifice is scarcely less deadly in the ideas and attitudes which it encourages. The cult of suffering is an extreme form of these; but even those who eschew this ultimately ambiguous attitude, are encouraged by the doctrine of redemption through sacrifice to propagate such falsehoods as the thesis that pain ennobles, to which I suspect

23

many of us give the lie each time we are overtaken by a dental abscess! Aristotle saw that men did best the things which they enjoyed doing, that zest for a task was an index of aptitude to its performance. Admittedly he underestimated the number of jobs any society demands which are both necessary and dull, requiring every sort of external incentive to make them bearable; (after all he gave a metaphysical account of the status of slavery). Yet these issues gain nothing through being sicklied over with the pale cast of chatter concerning vocation, especially vocation to sacrifice. To sacrifice ourselves is, it is said, to realize the image of the crucified, whereas the self-sacrificing may simply be mutilating himself, purposively destroying the sweetness of existence in the name of illusion, in order to make himself a hero in his own eyes.

To take one other illustration. Those who are familiar with the problems of the care of old people will know very well what I call the phenomenon of the "human sacrifice", the daughter in a large family who is described as "devoted to her parents" (the language has a ritual quality), and who is therefore chosen to look after them in their decline. Not infrequently she is the victim of various sorts of spiritual blackmail. Her patience perhaps is exhausted by her mother's near senile cantankerousness and she is told "you will be sorry one day dear, when I am dead and gone"; (and a discreet sob accompanies the last words). She sees her life slipping from her and still she is held in the vice-like grip, I will not say of dedication, but of convention consecrated by the ecclesiastical image of sacrifice. The ethic of sacrifice indeed provides a symbolism under which all sorts of cruelties may be perpetrated, not so much upon the weak as upon those who have been deceived by a false image of goodness. We need fresh air blown upon these discussions by a sane ethic of utility, properly designing the most humanly prudent course (in this case rational and human policies for the care of the aged), seeking to liberate human energies not to confine them.

> Theirs not to reason why;
> Theirs but to do or die.

The more fool they, a critical moralist might comment; and he would be right. It was Karl Barth, the greatest living theologian, who said to those Germans who in the immediate post-war years felt themselves cast for the role of the "suffering servant"—"it is not that you have been called to bear the suffering of the present time; it's simply that you have been political idiots". The matter was as simple as that; the German people had been politically inept with consequences under which our world still labours.

Yet to argue in this way is not to deny the extreme importance of the place of restraint in human life to which I earlier referred. We have to reckon today with what I can only describe as the cult of moral toughness, the belief that in personal morality men and women, who feel themselves strong enough to venture, are entitled to try everything, to ignore the elementary claims of others, to disdain the weak, to experiment with every sort of relationship. To confuse such disdain for the claims of restraint, and indeed of gentleness, with a true human freedom is simply to confuse with freedom a kind of superior strength, and to claim that what alone remains of justice is the right of those endowed with that strength to go their own way. Yet this strength reveals its counterfeit quality by the extent to which it reins in its ruthless energies in deference to such trivial concerns as good reputation. The connoisseur of sexual experiment and perversion, the seducer for whom all is fair game, the woman of affairs who eggs on a tired middle-aged husband to rejuvenate himself by lively sexual adventure, these types for all their toughness are curiously unwilling to risk ultimate damage to their own public reputations. Their ways are devious and they take care to move only in the twilight.

It would be a mistake however to suggest that practice of the kind of restraint and of respect for persons of which I have been speaking is today the prerogative of Christians (although Christian faith provides the kind of soil in which it should flourish). May I mention one recent outrage (I use the word advisedly) ? I refer to the publication of two volumes of personal letters by the late Dame Rose Macaulay to her spiritual adviser Father Hamilton Johnson of the Society of St John the Evangelist. These letters were never intended for publication; indeed their preservation might be thought due to the mistaken enthusiasm of a near-senile religious, although in my judgment his religious order cannot be exempted from blame in letting them see the light. The letters embody their author's reflections on religion, following a return to Anglican faith and practice after a long period during which she had had a prolonged affair with a married man who had eventually died. They are in no sense a record of her penitence for the outrage that quite conceivably she did to her lover's wife; in consequence by the triviality of much of their subject matter, they show a woman, entering after her lover was dead, into a cosy church world, where details of religious practice furnish endless topic for comment and conversation. Outrage is done not only by implication to the one whom it is hard to believe she did not injure, but to Miss Macaulay's own memory; for the writer of these letters, seems able only ceaselessly to discuss such topics as the variations of ceremonial practice between such London churches as the Grosvenor Chapel, St Paul's, Knightsbridge and the Annunciation, Bryanston Street. A reader, weary of these trivialities, may find himself, almost against his conscious will, echoing Anselm's words: *nondum considerasti quantum pondus sit peccatum.*

Whatever else we have here (and claim is made for the apologetic value of these letters, whatever that may mean) we have wanton disregard of the elementary duty of respect, of the kind of reverence that the sombre complexity of the human scene must always provoke. We have rather evidence of a sorry triviality of thought and feeling, indicating that what I have called restraint and respect are indeed necessary not simply to check the fierce indifference to the claims of others characteristic of the morally tough, but to prevent the currency of Christian conversation from being debased to the sorry level of most of these letters.

What however is disturbing pre-eminently in the manner in which Christian morality is presently commended is the way in which by its legalism, by its unself-critical attachment to the shibboleths of another world, by the poverty of its theological foundations, it leaves unraised crucial questions concerning the relations in human life of the elements of restraint and respect to those which are positive, which are indeed open because concerned with possibilities yet unknown. The humanist ethic at its most profound insists that the elements of restraint shall serve affirmative ends, and these ends are usually conceived in terms of the diminution of misery, the increase of human happiness, the enlargement of the opportunities open to human

28

kind. It is an ethic which exalts ends commending themselves to reason, over tradition; historically it has been the foe of cruelty, that most common fault of the servants of God in every age who by their fanatical devotion to the institution have so often betrayed themselves into the sort of mercilessness that, in the name of truth absolute, closes the gates of mercy on mankind. One has only to think of the moral enormities of the crusades to recall a classical instance of the temper I have in mind. In the January 1963 number of *The Twentieth Century* Mr Philip Toynbee suggests that, to a modern, cruelty rather than pride is the fundamental sin. It is certainly a characteristically ecclesiastical manifestation of pride to forget the pervasive cruelty of the servants of God, whose imaginative devotion is more often kindled by concern for the organisation and dignity of the community they serve than by any human concern for the delicate intricacies of personal existence. When one sees instances of the human misery caused by the hardness of prejudice in the Church one is reminded irresistibly that His Father's house was to be a house of prayer for all the nations. We do not in these islands today have to reckon with active persecutors; but we do have to reckon with those whose zeal for the status, repute, the orderliness of the Church (as they misguidedly conceive it) eclipses their readiness to receive the Son of Man when his call is apparent in the needs of the least of his brethren. We may seem here to have moved a long way from the horrors of the Albigensian crusade; but it is perhaps worthwhile to point a similar misunderstanding of the nature of God, of the Christian God, of whom after all Paul wrote that one who was in his form made himself of no reputation, and in that condescension to the manner of a servant revealed and defined for every age the essential nature of the divine.

If we say that the heart and marrow of Christian behaviour is love towards the brethren, we are still of course faced with the question what in practice this love involves. We can see that it counsels a kind of sharp impatience with the counterfeits of legalism, and moral legalism is indeed counterfeit morality; it constricts the substance of the good life in obedience to the traditions of historically relative human society. (It encourages for instance obsessional preoccupation with the "evils of divorce" to the exclusion of effective concern for the victims of broken marriages, and of support for those who often in great moral courage undertake to be husband or wife, let us say, to the innocent party in a broken marriage, and to serve her or him and the children of that first marriage, with heart-felt devotion. To experience ecclesiastically encouraged vindictiveness towards such persons, as I have done, is to be outraged that men who claim to speak of Christ's compassion should by their fanatic attachment to what they call the Church's moral law obscure his care for those who,

wounded by the attitude of his professed servants,
understandably deny the reality of that compassion.) Yet it is not enough to repudiate the
legalist perversion of the Christian way of behaviour; for the element of restraint is as we have seen
a crucially important element in a truly human
life and without it love may easily, will certainly,
plunge into a kind of vague sentimentality cruelly
indifferent to the facts of human injury and pain.
Moreover we have to reckon not with the troubled
image of the morally perplexed and bewildered,
whose fellows indeed we are, but with the self-
confident thrust of the morally tough, the strength
of the one who believes himself or herself to be
the stronger can masquerade as freedom; it is a
paradox that such strength can also take to itself
the name of love. But one can dispute that claim;
for that which is without gentleness, without
forbearance, can hardly claim to bear that
title.

May I return finally to the theological issues
which I raised? For Christians there is no escape
from the issues raised by the involvement of the
author and finisher of their faith in history. It is at
once their glory and their insecurity that he is so
involved. The very precariousness of our grasp
of his ways reflects the depth at which he pene-
trated the stuff of human life. We cannot have
that depth of identification on his part with our
circumstances unless we pay the price of the kind
of precariousness, belonging even to the sub-

stance of our faith, from which we may seek to run away to a spurious certainty even at the price of a kind of dishonesty which infects our whole outlook. We must be as sure as we can that we have rightly estimated the sort of certainty which we can hope to have about Jesus and do not make the mistake of trying to make that certainty other than it is.

Finally however if the Christian way of behaviour is to be liberated from the falsehoods and half-truths which beset it at so many levels it can so be set free only if the image of the crucified Lord, the author and finisher of our faith, is renewed. A false passivity, an invalid acquiescence in intolerable evils, a cultivation of obedience for obedience's sake, when revolt rather than acceptance is a plain human duty— these moral illusions have been fostered by misunderstanding of the work of Christ and dignified by the language of sacrifice, even of love. How are we to see that work in ways at once morally tolerable and morally revealing? The ways in which we are bidden see it, and indeed understand the divine plan to which it belongs, are in fact frequently morally intolerable; yet it is not enough to make of our understanding of the crucified something morally admissible; for here the Christian faces that which for faith is not of his own making. If he can reject all that diminishes its height and depth to dimensions less than the most profound he knows, it still concerns him that it should articulate for him questions from which he cannot turn aside.

We have in this lecture been largely concerned to criticize, angered perhaps by the crudities of so-called Christian moral teaching. Yet Christian morality remains a way of living which when it returns to contemplate its fontal inspiration is, in spite of all, uniquely able to hold together the claims of truth, of seeing things as they are or at least trying so to see them, and of mercy. The heart of the matter is here, and it is here because the cross supremely actualized that contradiction in human life, that splitting apart of the claim on the one side to call things, including evil things, by their name, and of mercy on the other. If Christ in his passion revealed to men the truth of what they are, we have to recall that he shrank from the work of that revelation. Some of you will know the hieratic representation of Christ the King, triumphantly arrayed in vestments at once ecclesiastic and temporal, recently fashionable in churches of a certain sort; but I hope a declining fashion. For such representations hardly do justice to the mockery and harrowing simplicity of the one of whom Pilate said *Ecce Homo*; yet this latter *is* the one who expresses in concrete human life, I will not say the reconciliation but rather, the endurance to the end of this contradiction. But it is to him that we must look, if our moral understanding is to be renewed, and it is in him that we must hope to find resources not confined in their power to illuminate the enclosed pathways of a cosy ecclesiastical tradition, but able to throw abundant light on the new ways that open before us, ensuring that we walk those ways in some conformity with the true pattern of our humanity.

PSYCHOLOGICAL OBJECTIONS

H. A. WILLIAMS

THE title of this lecture—Psychological objections to Christian belief—might suggest that my purpose is to criticize one orthodoxy, Christianity, by the dogmas of another orthodoxy, Psychology. But this would be an impossible task and for two reasons. The first reason can be stated simply in the short questions—What is Christianity? and, What is Psychology? For there is no agreed answer to either question. In the divided state of Christendom, Christianity can mean a great number of things. And even within one single Christian Communion, let us say the Roman Catholic Church, there are in practice considerable varieties of emphasis in what is held out for the contemplation of the faithful. The writings, for instance, of Dom Columba Marmion of the Order of St. Benedict are noticeably different in atmosphere from the writings of Teilhard de Chardin of the Society of Jesus. An apparent uniformity covers a considerable diversity—no bad thing unless life is bad. As for the world of psychology, it is as divided as Christendom. There are the well-known denominations—"I am of Freud", "I am of Jung", "I am of Pavlov", "I am of the half-subject psychology of the Natural Science Tripos Part I". And within these denominations there are, as within Christian denominations, varieties of emphasis. Although, for instance, Oedipus is theoretically fundamental in the Freudian mythology, the manner in which the myth is understood and applied in practice differs considerably from analyst to analyst. There can therefore be no question of treating Christianity and Psychology as though they were two fully defined and consistent systems of thought and seeing how one can criticize the other. We have not to do with two giants. On each side there is a variety of species.

But there is a more fundamental reason why it is impossible to match a Christian orthodoxy with a psychological orthodoxy—a reason more fundamental even than the fact that such monolithic orthodoxies do not exist. The second reason concerns the manner in which beliefs about human life and destiny are apprehended. We may imagine that it is a purely intellectual process, a matter of rigorous and consistent thinking. To think hard and to think clearly is all we need to apprehend the meaning of life. But is it? It would be absurd to underestimate the importance of giving intellectual form and content to our experience. Without doing so in some measure or other it would be impossible to live at all. But it would be equally absurd to separate the act of thinking from the person who thinks, or to claim that the thinker's dispositions and predilections, his good or bad fortune, the state of his health and the affairs of his heart will not effect the conclusions at which his thinking arrives. For man is not simply a thinking animal. He is an animal who feels and suffers. And what he feels and what he suffers will colour what he thinks. "All our reasoning" said Pascal, "All our reasoning reduces itself to yielding to feeling". Or in the words of Joseph Conrad in one of his later novels *Victory*— "The use of reason is to justify the obscure desires that move our conduct, to justify impulses, passions, prejudices and follies, and also our fears". But if what a man thinks is influenced by what he is, by what his past experience has made him, it would, in my opinion, be dishonest to set before you any system of ideas, be it labelled Christianity or Psychology, and claim for it an objective validity independent of my own subjective experience of living. I know that this is often done. To take an example from a field of study with which I am myself concerned—I know that the New Testament is often expounded as if the exposition were the product of pure scholarship alone. And I am sure that those who thus expound it honestly believe it to be the case. They do not see the looking-glass hidden in the pages of the text they are interpreting. It was Oscar Pfister, the Calvinist Pastor and Freudian analyst, in his book *Christianity and Fear* who said—"Tell me what you find in your Bible and I will tell you what sort of man you are". A similar warning has been given by Thomas Merton the Cistercian monk who now, after 15 years in a Trappist monastery, says this in his latest book *New Seeds of Contemplation*—"Our ideas about God tell us much more about ourselves than they do about God". What Pfister and Merton here say about religious beliefs could be applied to those who expound Psychology—"Tell me what you find in human nature and I will tell you what sort of man you are". There is no escape from this subjective element, although it can, of course, be denied, either explicitly or in the form and manner of presentation.

Let me now therefore say that all I can do this evening, under the grandiose title, Psychological Objections to Christian Belief, is to tell you of an inner conflict, a conflict which has arisen between, on the one hand, what I once believed to be essential elements of Christianity, and on the other, what I have discovered about the way I work as a human person, the subterranean forces and strategies of which I have become aware within. To many of you what I say may have little or no meaning. But this, I take it, is inevitable in all attempts at communication. The farmer, said Jesus, is not deterred by the knowledge that much of the seed he sows must of necessity be wasted. No claim is being made to any superiority of insight or to any store of esoteric knowledge. Psychology must not be regarded as the Gnosticism of the twentieth century. All that is being stated is the obvious—that I am not you and therefore our experience cannot be identical. But some of you may have had experience parallel with my own. Without coinciding it may overlap. So this lecture need not be a complete waste of time for everybody.

The inner conflict of which I spoke just now centres round an apparently inexhaustible capacity to disguise the truth from myself, to believe sincerely that I am doing one thing when in fact I am doing something quite different. If I may quote Conrad again (this time *Lord Jim*)—"It is my belief that no man fully understands his own artful dodges to escape from the grim shadow of self-knowledge". I agree with Conrad that the shadow *seems* grim, but that is because it is unknown, and we are frightened of the unknown as children are frightened of the dark. We prefer to bear, we fanatically insist on bearing those ills we have rather than fly to others that we know

39

not of. Yet such a death to the old self and rebirth to a new life has been the message of all the great religious geniuses down the centuries. And they have told us from their own experience, that it leads, not to the suspected ills, but to a richness and peace and abundant life unimaginable before. Yet the prospect of such a voyage of discovery terrifies us. Hence the artful dodges we employ to evade it. For some the artful dodges consist in work, for others pleasure, but the more respectable and praiseworthy the dodges appear to be, the more dangerously misleading they are. When Christianity is used as an artful dodge to allow me to escape from the discovery of what I am, when the light that is in me is thus darkness, how great is that darkness. And this, I believe, is what happens frequently. But before I speak in more general terms and in order to drive home the point, I want to tell you of something which actually happened to a man I know. Let us call him X. X was begining to question the validity of the continuous confessions of utter sinfulness and unworthiness which were a fundamental element of the Christianity in which he had been brought up. He went to a priest who told him that his questioning was the result of pride, an unwilling-ness to admit that he was a sinner. X was much comforted by this counsel and came away feeling at peace. But the peace of which he was conscious was interrupted by a series of dreams. X had a friend, Z, who was a sincere and much respected

Christian and who always laid great emphasis on the importance of self-abasement before God. Five or six times X dreamt that he met Z at a strip-tease show of the most degrading and illicit kind. These dreams told him nothing whatever, of course, about Z. But they told him something of immense importance about himself. In X's feelings, Z was associated with self-abasement before God. To dream several times of Z present at a degrading show was a clear indication that X's confessions of utter sinfulness were in fact a perverted form of lust. What appeared to be an element of sound Christianity, what was recommended on the authority of a priest, was thus in the end discovered by X to be an artful dodge to escape from the truth that an important part of him unhealthily enjoyed confessing sinfulness since it was a disguised indulgence in sexual perversion. When, at the start, he went to the priest and questioned the validity of self-abasement, he couldn't have said why he went. But clearly it was because he was beginning to grow out of his perversion. The priest's advice (which was sound enough theologically) gave him peace, since it represented permission to stay as he was and not move out of his sickness.

The practice of Christianity seems to me to be riddled with disguises of this sort. Christopher Isherwood, in his novel *The World in the Evening*, makes the hero say—"I believe in God but I hate the sort of people who do". I think what

Isherwood means is connected with these disguises. Suppose, for instance, that I were a writer who produced my best work during the time when I was having an illicit affair. Suppose the woman then died and I became a convert to some form of Christianity. I could repudiate my past as wholly wrong. Yet to it I must have owed some at least of the insight which enabled me to write so convincingly about the splendours and miseries of life. My repentance, partly genuine, is also partly me denying one of the sources of my inspiration, because in retrospect it now looks unattractive—like a dinner party one in fact enjoyed but which now, owing to an attack of jaundice, one cannot bear to think of. On one level, that is, consciously, I am responding to God's love. At the same time, I am also concealing from myself the fact that when God's love came to me as creative inspiration through the circumstances of my past, I am not humble enough to acknowledge it because of its unapproved and (as it seems to me now) ugly medium. It is as though my acceptance of the Christ, manifestly beautiful, were partly a disguise for my refusal to accept Him when He came self-emptied of His majesty, when (so it appears now), He had no form nor comeliness, and there was no beauty that we should desire Him. We were given a memorable and moving example of this situation in the lecture last week. Many Christians today believe that a second marriage after divorce brings with it the blessing and presence of Christ. Sixty years ago, almost all Christians would have opposed that belief to the death. The climate of opinion in our society has changed. Yet, sixty years ago, Christ would have been no less present in a second marriage, for all His being unrecognized by the pious, and, in general, despised and rejected. To deny Christ before men is not always the obvious thing it generally appears to be. Most of us have an enormous but unrealized vested interest in not recognizing Christ when he comes to us in forms which our culture and civilization disapprove. We allow ourselves to be too deafened by the music of the Church organ to hear Him say—"Why persecutest thou me?"

On the conscious level practising Christians are generally kind, forgiving, helpful, and apparently unselfish. But there is often something which doesn't quite ring true. Behind the consciously sincere generosity, there is often an egotism which is disturbing because it is unrecognized, and so, underhand. It is as though their Christianity were no more than a Merovingian Emperor. Behind stands the Mayor of the Palace whom they are too frightened to meet. The result is that what they honestly consider to be serving God for his own sake is really a making use of God to serve themselves. They use Him chiefly as the whitewash with which to paint the sepulchre where their own corruption lies concealed. The impression left is of something

43

surreptitious. So the kindly smile sickens and the helping hand depresses. And one is left feeling— "This is not *you* doing this at all. *You* are really doing something else, trying to buy a couple of ounces of pious feeling, although of course you don't know it". In short there is a lack of that spontaneity which is of the essence of charity. By way of contrast consider a character in a novel I hope you have all read—Randall Peronett in Iris Murdoch's *An Unofficial Rose*. Randall is in the usual sense of the word as selfish as hell. He leaves his wife and daughter and goes off with another woman without the slightest regard for the suffering this is bound to cause. Now please don't think I am advocating this sort of behaviour. All I want to point out is that Randall did not shelter behind any disguise. He did not hide from himself the sort of man he was or the sort of thing he was doing. He met himself and accepted what he found. And by thus being him, in spite of his deplorable behaviour, he gave. Just by being, without any pretences, the man who was Randall Peronett, he gave to the very wife he deserted. And so much did he thus give her that she, without having any but the dimmest idea of what she was doing, concluding merely that real compassion is agnosticism, awaited his return. It is those who shed disguises who inspire devotion, because what they offer is something real, even if they behave as badly as Randall did.

44

Or consider two better known characters, Simon the Pharisee in St Luke's gospel and the uninvited guest who appeared at his table—the prostitute. So overlaid was Simon with official piety that he had killed within him the spontaneity of love. The uninvited guest had not. She was herself, and being so, was still capable of loving. At times it had led her to walk the streets, but it also brought her to the feet of Jesus. Simon, the good churchman, was dead. The woman was alive. And Jesus said of her—"Her sins which are many are forgiven because she loved much". Now I know that devotees of what Mr E. M. Forster has called the suburban Jehovah have tried to save St Luke, have tried to save Jesus Himself, from saying that the woman's sins were forgiven because she loved much. Instead Jesus is made to say—her great love shows she has been forgiven. But as Dr R. P. Casey pointed out in the Classical Review, this translation forces the Greek intolerably. (Incidentally both James Moffatt and the Revised Standard Version give the old and natural rendering). Translating to make Jesus say what middle-class Christian dons consider suitable is not without its humorous aspect. It is a good example of the limitations of learning.

The sort of spontaneity shown by the woman who was a sinner is not encouraged by Christian pastors. They generally help us to hide from what we are by telling us to decide to be something else.

45

We are always being told to make decisions—to decide for Christ, to decide to be forgiving, to decide to die to self. But real decisions are never calculated or thought out in this way. They mature by themselves as a tree grows. The earth beareth fruit of herself. If, for instance, I make a conscious decision to be humble, I don't become humble. I become what Blake called sneaking— the type which Dickens caricatured in Uriah Heep, although of course I do it much better than Uriah (I hope). This is the result of my never going deep enough into myself to discover the real cause of my aggressiveness. So the engine of aggressiveness races on as before. But what it produces is no longer open and above board. Instead it produces an extremely strained meekness and mildness. I go about like a melodramatic stage version of the Lamb of God and the Suffering Servant rolled into one. "That is the path we all choose" said George Eliot "when we set out on the abandonment of our egotism—the path of martyrdom and endurance where the palm-branches grow". The real aggression which supplies me with the props and paint for this performance makes itself felt through the disguise. And because it is underhand, it hits below the belt. It is destructive of the people on whom it is exercised in a way in which open aggression never is. Such consciously contrived humility might almost be called a diabolical perversion of aggression. Bernard Shaw's epigram is applicable to the grown-up as well as to the young—"Never strike a child except in anger". Yet Christians are often so pathologically intent on preserving as far as they can an image of themselves as Christ-like, that they are totally unaware of the harm their attempted humility is doing to other people.

I said "pathologically intent" deliberately. Psychopathology consists in a limited awareness of what I am combined with a dogged determination to preserve this limited vision at all costs. Part of the game, of course, is not to realize this fact. I go to Church, I read the Bible, I say my prayers, I do good works, I become a clergyman, in order to keep what I am at arm's length, draping a curtain between it and my eyes. Job did this. Job was a righteous man who hid from himself. Then God stripped everything from him. The result was at first self-pity. This in time gave way to the horrors. What was revealed to Job was terrifying because it was utterly destructive of what Job thought he was. But the reality he saw with such terror destroyed only what Job thought he was. It did not destroy Job. On the contrary, it gave him himself. Not a Job who could claim to be the captain of his own soul, especially in the obedience he gave to God's will. But a Job, who by means of terror, saw and was satisfied. "I heard of thee by the hearing of the ear, but now my eyes see thee; therefore I despise myself and repent in dust and ashes". What Job despised, what he repented of in dust and ashes, was the good, God-fearing, religious Job of the early chapters, the Job who was blind, who heard about God and imagined he served him, but who in fact had never seen him. The vision which made Job into himself and destroyed what Job thought he was, this vision was not contrived. For it was precisely the Job of the early chapters who was set on contriving, contriving to be moral and religious. And this contriving for all its apparent praiseworthiness, was really a disguise for the successful attempt to preserve his blindness. What happened then was beyond his control. God shook him upside down and turned him inside out, so much so that Job wished he were dead and cursed the day on which he was born. But the final result was a genuine death to a false image of himself and a genuine birth to what he really and fully was.

Now compare the drama of Job with what the churches generally say about repentance and rebirth. Stop doing a, b, c. Tell God you are sorry for doing them and start trying to do x, y, and z. The possibility of vision is excluded from the start. The path of increasing awareness is blocked. And if something within me tells me this is so, if a voice within hints that I am being disloyal to what I truly am—well, such things are never felt explicitly or articulated in any clear message. I merely feel that being a Christian is being a strain, and for that complaint the clergyman has

an answer ready to hand. Jesus told us it would
be difficult to follow Him. It is such an easy,
plausible and seductive lie. Last June there was
an article in The Sunday Times by the Rector
of Woolwich, the Reverend Nicholas Stacey, in
which he said that more often than not the
fundamental reason why young people are not
Christians is a sin which they are not honest
enough to know would have to be given up.
Stacey seemed to be totally unaware of the
absolutely sincere and agonizing conflict of
loyalties which must come to those who are seeking the truth about themselves. To give up what
Stacey calls a sin in order to toe the line to a
prefabricated pattern of behaviour may be the
very sin against the Holy Ghost. For the apparent
goodness of such a submission is a disguise for an
evasion, a refusal to run the risk and incur the
possible terror of discovering the real evil of
which I am the slave, an evasion made possible
by my accepting as evil and so giving up what the
moral establishment dictates. Throw out the
painted icon of the devil in my room, in order that
the devil himself can stay put, securely invisible.
"Straight is the gate and narrow is the way"
said Jesus, "which leadeth unto life, and few
there be that find it". The churches generally
preach something different—"Few there be who,
having found it, have the moral courage to walk
on it or remain walking on it. For it is easy enough
to find. It is plain for all to see". The ease and

49

certainty with which the churches point to the road and their assumption that it is obvious to all men of good will leads me to think that the road they thus recommend is not the narrow way at all, but the wide gate and the broad way which leads to destruction.

The weapon with which the churches bludgeon me on to the broad way is that of inflating the feelings of guilt which lie latent in us all. Make a person feel guilty enough and he will do what he is told. This latent guilt-feeling is a non-rational sense of a harshly authoritative figure who judges and condemns us. It is as though the external authoritative figures we have known all our lives have been injected inside us like a virus and have in this way become part of ourselves. If we think God exists, these feelings of a harsh pitiless authority get associated with Him, however much our conscious reason insists that God is Love. Even if, shall we say, a man is a Christian Theologian of the highest calibre, it is still possible for him to feel the inner Juggernaut, and in his feelings to confuse the Juggernaut with God. What H. G. Wells' Mr Polly thought of God we educated people do not think of Him. But there can be very few of us indeed who do not sometimes in a confused way *feel* God to be as Mr Polly considered Him—"A limitless Being having the nature of a schoolmaster and making infinite rules, known and unknown, rules that were always ruthlessly enforced and with an infinite capacity for punishment, and, most horrible of all to think of, limitless powers of espial." Now it is not at all difficult to whip up this unholy ghost inside us and make him active. There is a great deal wrong with the world, and the ghost can be made to tell us that it is largely our fault. I remember a preacher making us feel that it was our selfishness which helped to cause the 1914 war, although most of us had not been born until after the armistice had been signed. But of course it is generally done with greater subtlety than that, although the object aimed at is the same, to make us feel shabby, mean, contemptible, monstrously ungrateful to the God who made us. And so the unholy ghost within us is set furiously to work. He is what William Blake called the Nobodaddy—Nobody's daddy, He who is not. Even mild, gentlemanly, sober, cautious, exhortations about sin give Nobodaddy his opportunity. In Blake's words—"The Nobodaddy aloft farted and belched and coughed". And the result is we feel it absolutely necessary to placate him. And here is the deadly opportunity for effective evangelism. We have been brought under old Nobodaddy's spell, and towards him we insinuate, flatter, bow and bend the knee. (If you want to know what I mean read Cranmer's two general confessions in the Book of Common Prayer.) But hope is offered to us. We shall be saved if we do what we are told. This may be giving up a sin or practising a virtue. It may be the performance of religious exercises. It may be singing "Just as I am without one plea", and "I am all unrighteousness". Nobodaddy's fury subsides. We have shown the white flag and capitulated to Him. Peace is declared. But the peace is bought with a price. And the price is my destruction. For what I am and what I do is no longer the activity of a free agent. I am the slave of my own guilt-feelings, reduced to a puppet manipulated by this horrific puppeteer.

Let me now give you an actual example of what I have been describing. I know a man—he was a person of some academic intelligence—who was loyally practising his religion as a devout and rather high church Anglican. One night he had a nightmare which proved to be a turning point in his life. In his dream he was sitting in a theatre watching a play. He turned round and looked behind him. At the back of the theatre there was a monster in human form who was savagely hypnotizing the actors on the stage, reducing them to puppets. The spectacle of this harsh inhuman puppeteer exercising his hypnotic powers so that the people on the stage were completely under his spell and the slaves of his will— this spectacle was so terrifying that the man awoke trembling and in a cold sweat. After several months he gradually realized that the monster of the nightmare was the god he was really worshipping in spite of his having got a First in the Theological Tripos. And to this god he had painfully to die. He had to accept the terrible truth that the practice of his religion had been a desperate attempt to keep his eyes averted from the monster of the nightmare. He had thought that, with many failures, it is true, but according to his powers, he was responding to God's love. His dream showed him that he was a devil's slave—his devotion and his goodness being a compulsive response to a deeply embedded feeling of guilt, and this, in spite of his regular use of sacramental confession. It broke him up temporarily. But later he was certain that, although he was much less religious in the usual sense, he had been brought to the straight gate and narrow way. For life and behaviour based on feelings of guilt excludes charity. To be bullied, compelled, by subtle inner unidentifiable fear to apparent worship and goodness is to destroy the self. And without a self one cannot give. There can be no charity, no love for God or man. The dreamer whose history (with his permission) I have recounted was seen, about two years after his nightmare, drunk among the bars and brothels of Tangier. He was learning that for him evil was not what the priests had told him it was, but rather that evil was the disguised slavery to his own hidden corruption which had led him to go to Mass every day and to confession every month. And he told me that words of Jesus rang in his ears like bells of victory—the words which Jesus addressed to the churchmen of His day—"Verily

53

I say unto you, That the publicans and the harlots go into the Kingdom of God before you". Now I am not suggesting that it is a good or morally desirable thing to spend one's time drunk among the bars and brothels of any city. What I am suggesting with all the emphasis at my command is that there are worse, much worse, evils than that. Worse because unperceived and thus sincerely imagined to be good. If you are the slave of drink or sex, somewhere inside you, you know you are a slave. But if you are the slave of guilt-feelings, you can deceive yourself and call it the service of God or even free response to God's love. That is why a congregation of "good" people in church can be much further from the heart of God than those who have strayed from the path of conventional behaviour. "They that are whole" said Jesus "have no need of the physician. But they that are sick!" As a matter of straightforward historical fact it is true that Jesus of Nazareth was not crucified by the publicans and sinners. He was crucified by the Church. And here some words of Bishop Charles Gore should haunt us in season and out—"I see nowhere any ground for believing that the officers under the New Covenant would be protected from error, if they should behave like the officers under the Old". As Reinhold Niebuhr said here in Cambridge twenty years ago—"The Church can be Anti-

Christ, and if and when the Church fails to admit this, it is the Anti-Christ."

I believe that behind the outwardness of much worship and good works there lies a fact which Christians unknowingly do all in their power to keep hidden from their eyes—the fact that they have sold themselves as slaves to the demon of guilt-feelings, however much intellectually they refuse the idea and however enlightened their theology of the atonement. For what we really believe is often very different from what we think we believe.

One final comment seems worth making. It follows from what I have said, and is about the authority of the New Testament. St Paul and St John were men of like passions to ourselves. However great their inspiration, however much they could soar into regions where we could not even begin to follow, being human, their inspiration was not even or uniform. Sometimes, like all other men, they knew not of what spirit they were. For with their inspiration went that degree of psychopathology which is the common lot of all men. They too had their inner axes to grind of which they were unaware. What therefore they tell us must have a self-authenticating quality, like music. If it doesn't, we must be prepared to refuse it. We must have the courage to disagree. But what then of the Jesus of the synoptic gospels? Some at least of his words must have been altered in tone and emphasis by the communities which handed them on before they were written down. The first Christian communities were not lacking in impulses, passions, prejudices, follies and fears. And these, without any deliberate dishonesty, must sometimes have coloured their account of what Jesus said. So His words for us must have their own inherent authority. There is surely no difficulty here. A play is not good because it is held to have been written by Shakespeare. Its quality is self-evident. So it must be with the recorded words of Jesus. Sometimes we must reject as untrue and unworthy a sentiment He is reported to have held. In practice it will be discovered that this still leaves us with incalculable riches.

HISTORICAL
OBJECTIONS

A. R. VIDLER

T HE purpose of these lectures
is neither to substantiate nor to refute objections
to Christian belief, but to offer you some assis-
tance in thinking out for yourself what is involved
in Christian belief. That means reckoning as
openly and honestly as possible with what can be
said against it as well as with what can be said
for it. What I design to do therefore in this
lecture is to set before you some considerations
that I think you ought to take into account when
assessing the relation between Christian belief
and history. But "history" and "historical" are
large and elusive terms: almost anything could
come within their embrace. I shall concentrate

57

on that range of questions which has to do with the supposed dependence of Christian belief on what has actually happened not in history in general, but in a particular bit of history.

Christianity is an historical faith not only in the banal sense that it has by now had a long history, but in that it seems to require belief in the occurrence of certain quite specific events in the past. This claim was recently made in an unequivocal manner by Professor Mascall in his inaugural lecture at King's College, London, when he said:

> It has often been emphasized that Christianity is historical in a sense in which no other religion is, for it stands or falls by certain events which are alleged to have taken place during a particular period of forty-eight hours in Palestine nearly two thousand years ago.

And he quoted the late Dom Gregory Dix as having said that Christianity "is the only fully historical religion. It is the only religion which actually *depends entirely upon* history . . ."

I am not—at any rate at this stage—expressing agreement or disagreement with those statements. I cite them only in order to indicate the central topic of this lecture. I am sure that another lecturer with other interests and a greater competence might discourse in a big way about "the philosophy of history" or about objections to the idea that there is a Christian philosophy of

58

history. That larger, though perhaps less crucial, subject is not within my scope.

First, I would call your attention to a fundamental objection to any tie-up between Christian belief and alleged historical events or the existence of an historical person. Here are a few examples:

Goldsworthy Lowes Dickinson (both his bed-maker and his biographer—E. M. Forster—felt he was the best man who ever lived) said this:

> My difficulty about Christianity is and always has been that Christians make the centre of their faith the historical existence of a man at a certain age. I dare say he *did* exist, though that has been doubted. But if he *did*, what was he really like? I cannot think religion can depend on such uncertainties.

A similar objection was expressed by the Mahatma Gandhi in an address which he gave—oddly enough—on Christmas Day 1931:

> I may say that I have never been interested in an historical Jesus. I should not care if it was proved by some one that the man called Jesus never lived, and that what was narrated in the Gospels was a figment of the writer's imagination. For the Sermon on the Mount would still be true for me.

Again, Sir Walter Raleigh, who was Professor of English at Oxford, wrote to his sister in 1899:

59

I send you a book which I believe to be by Bernard Holland—piejaw in its nature, about Churches and religion and the like . . . Much as I like Bernard, I get further and further from that point of view. All these questions are very interesting (and well treated by him) so long as you remain inside Christianity, but I can't stay there. It seems absurd to subordinate philosophy to certain historical events in Palestine—more and more absurd to me, I think. The *ideas* of Christianity are always interesting, but they are all to be found elsewhere, and are not, it would seem, the chief part of its attraction.

My last example is a more trivial one—from Bernard Shaw—but it also has its point:

What Christ said would have been just as true if he had lived in a country house with an income of £5,000 a year.

None of these men was a professing Christian, but they might all (except perhaps Shaw) be described as sympathetic or regretful dissenters. You will observe however that they all considered that Christian belief ought to be about the teaching, not the person, of Jesus. They considered that Jesus happened to enunciate certain spiritual and moral truths, ideals or principles the validity of which was independent of his own person or circumstances, just as it is not necessary to know anything about the biography of Bach in order to be pierced to the soul by his music. It is the music, not the man, that matters. It is the teaching of the Sermon on the Mount, not who uttered it, that matters. Well, you have to ask yourself with regard to Christian belief whether or not that is so: whether or not Christians have been misguided in identifying their beliefs with affirmations about particular historical events.

It is the same point as was made in a more abstract way by Lessing in the eighteenth century when he said that:

> If no historical truth can be demonstrated, then nothing can be demonstrated by historical truths. That is to say, accidental truths of history can never become the proof of necessary truths of reason.

Lessing was a professing Christian, and there have been Christians since who have so interpreted Christian belief as to make its justification independent of the question whether or to what extent the events recorded in the New Testament actually occurred. This, if I understand him aright, is the position of Professor Braithwaite in his lecture, *An Empiricist's View of the Nature of Religious Belief.* "A religious belief," he says, "is an intention to behave in a certain way . . . together with the entertainment of certain stories associated with the intention in the mind of the believer." "A man is not, I think, a professing Christian unless he both proposes to live according to Christian moral principles and associates his intention with thinking of Christian stories; but he need not believe that the empirical propositions presented by the stories correspond to empirical fact." A similar view was expressed at the beginning of this century by one of the Roman Catholic modernists—not by all of them, as is often alleged, not for example by Loisy or Tyrrell, but—by Édouard Le Roy who like Braithwaite was a lay professor. Le Roy, who became a member of the Académie Française and died only in 1954—taught that Christian dogma is primarily a rule of practical conduct.

The professional theologians have not taken kindly to these views which, it is urged, could never "constitute an effective basis of missionary propaganda". It is suggested that they can appeal only to sophisticated and sceptically inclined academics. I am not so sure about that. I fancy that there are a great many ordinary Christian believers who, if they were articulate, would confess that it is the *practical* implications of Christian belief which are of decisive importance for them, and not the historical origins or the *speculative* implications. So I do not think that we should let the professional theologians too swiftly dissuade us from considering these views seriously. And I notice that the present Dean of St Paul's has gone so far as to say: "I see no reason to suppose that a complete abandonment of the historical basis for Christianity would necessarily involve the end of the religion," though I should add that he was speaking only of an extreme hypothesis, and not of one that he is himself in the least disposed to entertain.

For, after all, there can be no doubt that Christian teachers and preachers as a whole, and the vast majority of Christian worshippers, take it for granted that their faith is inescapably bound up with what actually happened in Palestine in the first century of our era and that, as has been said, "the Gospel, divorced from its basis in history, must needs lose its essential power". I therefore turn to consider more precise objections to Christian belief thus understood, the difficulties that are entailed in it, and ways in which attempts have been made to meet them.

On the one hand, it can be claimed that Christian belief derives its peculiar strength and interest from its affirmation that the eternal God, who is the ground of all being, once upon a time and once for all not only disclosed himself but in "the flesh", that is, in the concrete stuff of our human existence, initiated for mankind a universal movement of healing and restoration—a new creation. This affirmation, it is claimed, sharply distinguishes Christian belief from any assertion of general ideas or timeless principles, from mere guidance for conduct, and from suggestive mythologies: and this it was that enabled Christianity in the early centuries to triumph over the faiths that were competing with it.

On the other hand, it must be recognized that this claim to be rooted in, and to derive from, actual historical events exposes Christian belief to objections or to doubts which have become more acute in the last century or two since scientific methods of historical investigation have established themselves. This was acknowledged by Dr H. M. Relton in an essay on "The Reconstruction of Dogma":

> The appeal of Christianity is still, and must always be, an appeal to history. This cannot be helped. There must always, therefore, be an element of doubt and query. Did these things really happen? There must always be room for critical investigation, and a right employment of the historical method must always be welcomed.

(By the way, why does he say "a *right* employment of the historical method"? Does he mean one that sees to it that the answers come out right?) I prefer the way the point has been made more recently by Mr Christopher Driver:

> Because Christianity is a historical religion, because Christians are ever charged with seeking the truth about the created world and the begotten Christ, the Church is singularly vulnerable to the advancement of knowledge.

In what respects then is Christian belief historically vulnerable?

First, Christians are expected to hold their

beliefs with such assurance that they are prepared
not only to live by them but, if necessary, to die
for them. But, if we look closely into the question,
we have to acknowledge that no beliefs about
matters of history can be proved to be certainly
true: strictly speaking, they can never have more
than a very high degree of probability. Do
Christians then live and die for what they must
allow to be not certainly, but only probably, the
case?

Some Christians have a way of meeting this
objection which is not open to me. They grant
that what I have said is correct about historical
statements in general, but they say that Christian
beliefs involving matters of history are presented
to us in a form which lifts them altogether above
the uncertainties of historical evidence. They
come to us with a guarantee of certainty either
in an infallible book or from an infallible pope
or both. If that claim could be sustained in either
form, we should not need to bother any more
about arguments from history and that is why
Cardinal Manning said that "the appeal to
antiquity is both a treason and a heresy: it is
treason because it rejects the divine voice of the
Church at this hour, and a heresy because it
denies that voice to be divine". In that case, it
would be unnecessary for me to proceed with this
lecture. However, even if such claims could be
sustained (and I do not think they can be), I
should disregard them here, for in these lectures

65

we are appealing not to any supernatural or miraculous authority but to reason. I therefore proceed.

Anyhow, the objection that historical statements can never be certainly demonstrated is not so formidable as it may seem. Christians do not assert, or they never ought to assert, that the truth of their beliefs can be demonstrated with certainty. If that were so, they would no longer be beliefs but knowledge. Christians would no longer be walking by faith but by sight. This is of course an intricate subject which depends to some extent on the definition of words. All I need point out here is the distinction, which is often overlooked, between the logical certainty of propositions and the psychological certitude of persons: between saying "it is certain" and "I am certain". Every day of our lives we all show that we are practically or psychologically certain about things which we could not demonstrate to be certainly true—at least, not if we were cross-examined by any competent philosopher.

The objection, so broadly stated, does not therefore hold, but it leads to an objection with a much sharper point. It must be granted that it is quite reasonable for persons to be certain about matters which cannot be certainly demonstrated, including historical statements such as that William the Conqueror came over in 1066. But that is so, either because there is universal agreement about the beliefs in question except among lunatics, or because we have adequate grounds for supposing that if we ourselves examined the evidences we should find them convincing. But do these conditions hold in the case of the historical statements involved in Christian belief?

Obviously they are not matters of universal agreement: in fact, the early Christians were regarded as mad because they believed them, and it has often been so since. What then about examining the evidences for ourselves? It would not be reasonable to expect every Christian, or non-Christian for that matter, to be competent to examine the evidences concerning the origins of Christianity and to reach dependable conclusions about them on the ground of his own inquiries. This is an undertaking that calls for exceptional philological, literary, critical and historical expertise. It would be unreasonable, I say, to require people to become trained historians or critical experts before they could become Christians or before they could renounce Christian belief.

In this, as in many other matters, we most of us have to depend more or less upon the experts. But here is the difficulty. It is well enough known that the experts—those who have made themselves competent to form an opinion of their own about Christian origins—differ very widely in their conclusions. There have even been learned and intelligent men who have denied that Jesus ever existed: the so-called "Christ-myth" theory. However, by the generality of even radically sceptical critics, that is regarded as a fantasy of criticism. You must always bear in mind the words of Ronald Balfour in his essay on "History" in *Cambridge University Studies:*

> Facts can be found which will support almost any historical thesis, and the more learned the historian the more of such facts he will be able to cite.

But apart from the extravagance of the Christ-myth theory, why is it that experts in this field differ so widely from one another? For one thing, while it may seem to undergraduates who are reading for the theological tripos that the documentary records of Christian origins are pretty substantial and extensive, yet in comparison with the import of their subject-matter they are all too fragmentary. I remember an eminent New Testament scholar saying to me that the period before A.D. 170 is rather like the prehistory of Christianity, and that we have sufficient documentation for a history proper only after that date. I think there is something in that analogy. It does not of course mean that we can reach no conclusions about the earlier period, but the comparative fragmentariness of the surviving records accounts in part for the variety of ways in which they can be interpreted.

There is indeed a remarkable coherence in the New Testament as a whole: it is not for nothing that the books it contains are bound up together.

At the same time, they are in many respects heterogeneous; there are striking inconsistencies between them; there was evidently a process of development or evolution going on during the period when they were being composed; there is considerable uncertainty about when exactly most of them should be dated. All these circumstances go far to explain the different conclusions which experts reach, or their hesitation in arriving at any firm conclusions.

But there are other factors that must be taken into account. It is the case that some historians are by temperament more sceptically inclined or more cautious than others, not only in this but in other fields of study. While there are some who, when they have made up their minds, will write with great confidence and aplomb, others persist in qualifying even their most considered or cherished conclusions with such expressions as "probably", "possibly", "perhaps", "it may seem", or "it would appear". The late Professor R. H. Lightfoot of Oxford was an agreeable example of this habit of mind. One needs to make allowance for this personal equation when estimating the significance of disagreement between experts.

However, a much more important question is that of *bias*. Presumably, we should all like to feel that our favourite historians were unbiassed. But the question is: can they really be so? Allow them the maximum of honesty: but can they really approach a subject without any presuppositions in their minds? The best and most balanced treatment of this question that I know of is in the essay which I referred to just now by Ronald Balfour in *Cambridge University Studies*. Broadly speaking, it must be said that, while it is impossible for a historian to be completely without bias or completely presuppositionless, there is a vitally important difference between those historians who appear to be making out a case for conclusions which they hold in advance, and those who are genuinely wanting the evidences to speak for themselves, who seek to discount their own bias, and who are manifestly willing, if need be, to reach conclusions that are uncongenial to them.

This brings me to a graver objection and I am always surprised that more is not made of it. For have you observed that, in Cambridge for example, those scholars who are deemed competent to give teaching about Christian origins are almost without exception (indeed, so far as I know, without any exception) committed members of Christian Churches, whether as ministers or lay men (which is only a matter of degree), although this is not a formal condition of their appointment? This is not the case everywhere, especially in some continental universities, which may explain why there is much more variety in the teaching that is given there. But in England it has been said that the teaching of theology, and

this includes the elucidation of Christian origins,
is mostly carried on within the sound of church
bells. In our Divinity School in St John's Street
the bells of Great St Mary's can be clearly heard,
and even the solitary bell of King's College
Chapel, as I know very well since I sometimes
depart from a meeting in the Divinity School
when I hear that bell start ringing!

Renan in the preface to his *Vie de Jésus* likened
orthodox theologians to caged birds and liberal
theologians to birds whose wings have been
clipped. He meant that, when theologians study
the historical evidences for the life of Jesus or
for anything else that bears on their creed, they
are tied down in advance by the dogmas to which
they are committed. Liberal theologians may
appear to fly a little way in the direction to which
the evidences point them, but they are not really
free to do so. Now I must say that I am not myself
sensible of being either caged or clipped or
inhibited from saying what I really think by my
ministry or membership in a church, and anyhow
Renan was ill-qualified to say this kind of thing
since he laid it down as an axiom of his own
thinking that miracles cannot happen, which is a
thoroughly unphilosophical presupposition. But
although I myself feel free to think and say whatever I believe to be true, and while I have the
highest opinion of the honesty and integrity of
my colleagues in the Divinity Faculty here, I
should be happier if those who are appointed to

give teaching about Christian origins in this university were less apparently tarred with a bias. I have very much sympathy with an article on this subject by Professor Ninian Smart in the December 1962 issue of the *Universities Quarterly*.

But there is more involved in this question of presuppositions than we have so far considered. What range of evidence may rightly be taken into account and influence our decision when making up our minds whether or not the hard core of the Christian story is to be accepted, for I apprehend that Christians need have no difficulty in granting that there may be legendary embellishments of the story even in the canonical gospels? There are some—both believers and unbelievers—who suppose that you can more or less isolate the story of Jesus, and even particular incidents in it, and treat it somewhat like a detective story—what Mark Pattison once called the "Old Bailey" type of theology. An example of this is that book by Frank Morison, *Who Moved the Stone?*, in which he starts as an unbeliever and arrives at an orthodox conclusion.

I do not myself find such books convincing or at any rate decisive, whatever conclusion they come to, because they presuppose that you can make up your mind about the story of Jesus without viewing it in its total context, in particular without taking into account the Old Testament of which it purports to be the fulfilment, and without taking into account the subsequent

history of the Christian movement. As regards
the latter, Dr Relton has written:

Investigation of the historicity of Christianity cannot be confined (he means "ought not
to be confined") to an inquiry concerning
events of (Christ's) earthly life without any
reference to the phenomenon of the Christian
Church which arose as a result of that life, and
claims still to live in the power of His endless
life.

This point was put with a sharper accent by
another English divine (Alfred Fawkes):

The question of origin, so fiercely discussed
by theologians, is in truth the least decisive of
questions; the point is not what a formula, a
function, an institution was, but what it has
become. This, not the other, fixes at once its
worth and its character.

It seems reasonable, and indeed inevitable,
that a man's judgment about the origins of
Christianity—where the evidences in the narrower sense are manifestly susceptible of more than
one interpretation—should be influenced by his
assessment of the total Christian phenomenon in
history. I do not say that this will make it any
easier—at any rate, for a detached observer—to
make up his mind. For the Christian movement
in history has a brighter and a darker side.
As regards the brighter side I will cite the

73

testimony not of a Christian, who might be starry-eyed in the matter, but of that famous agnostic T. H. Huxley:

> Whoso calls to mind what I may venture to term the bright side of Christianity—that ideal of manhood, with its strength and patience, its justice and its pity for human frailty, its helpfulness to the extremity of self-sacrifice, its ethical purity and nobility, which apostles have pictured, in which armies of martyrs have placed their unshakable faith, and whence obscure men and women, like Catherine of Siena and John Knox, have derived courage to rebuke Popes and Kings—is not likely to underrate the importance of the Christian faith as a factor in human history.

But against that we have to set the darker aspects of Christian history: the quarrelsomeness of the Christians, their intolerance, their censoriousness, their legalism, their arrogance, the blatant immorality of doctrines which they have accepted with equanimity, and the Christian Church's all too frequent resemblance to the Jewish Church which crucified Christ.

Possibly a distinction may be drawn here, as is done by Dr Emil Brunner, between the Christian *Ekklesia* by which he means the communities of believers who have lived in the Spirit of Jesus and who have taken him at his word, and the Church as a great hierarchical, juridical, quasi-political organization, which has been animated by a very different spirit. It is only of the former that even a detached observer might be moved to say that at the bottom of this phenomenon there may have been or there must have been some stupendous event which was not of this world. But on the other hand he might equally well be moved to say that this is the evasion of a clever theologian who is trying to have the best of both worlds!

I have been speaking of a "detached observer", and I am sure that it is good for all of us— whether we are believers or unbelievers—to try to look at Christianity sometimes from that point of view. But of course in reality we are, none of us, detached observers. We are inevitably involved or engaged in one way or another, and influenced by the experiences we have had and the decisions we have made heretofore.

So that, finally, I would say that the way in which a Christian believer responds, in the last resort, to the historical objections to Christian belief which we have been considering is likely to be settled by one or both of two things, which are not unrelated. On the one hand, by the enduring impression or impact that is made upon him by the person of Jesus as he is portrayed in the Gospels. It is by no means easy to get at this because—apart from the fact that there are extraneous elements even in the Gospel records— the Christians themselves have so mucked up the impression of Jesus—by all that Sunday School

75

silliness about "Jesus meek and gentle", or by turning him into a cleric or an idealist, or by concealing him behind an elaborate façade of dogma, or by those distressing pictures in stained glass windows which were beloved by the Victorians and have yet to be smashed. All the same the authentic personality of Jesus does still make its impact. As an example of its doing so today, I would recommend a recently published paperback by Roger Tennant, entitled *Son of a Woman*. Here you have a man with a genuinely post-Darwinian, post-Marxist, post-Freudian mind, who has also knocked about the world a lot, and who has found the person of Jesus inescapable.

And, on the other hand, whether a man decides to become or to remain a Christian believer may also be settled by what I would call his participation in the Christian mystery as a present reality: by what he finds, or by what finds him, in the shared experience of the community of believers —it may be in the eucharistic sacrament or in the Friends' meeting house: by whether or not he is convinced that there is something there which, despite all his puzzlements, holds him and speaks to the deepest levels of his being. This, I take it, is what Paul Tillich had in mind when he said:

> The affirmation that Jesus is the Christ is an act of faith and consequently of daring courage. It is not an arbitrary leap into darkness but a decision in which elements of immediate parti-

cipation and therefore certitude are mixed with elements of strangeness and therefore incertitude and doubt.

I want to end with a word first to the non-Christians, and then to the Christians, and then to both. To the non-Christians I would say, make sure that you are considering the objections to your own beliefs or unbeliefs as searchingly as the Christians are in these lectures being pressed to consider the objections to their beliefs. And here I might interject that I often find myself more in sympathy or *en rapport* with non-Christians who have a sense of the strangeness and incertitude of our world and of the duty of a large measure of agnosticism than I do with Christians who are cocksure about their beliefs.

And to the Christians I would say: don't expect or require that all Christians should see eye to eye about these matters. Don't try to lay down a hard and fast line between what are the essentials and the non-essentials of belief, for that is one of the questions that will be with us till the end of time. And don't expect to require all Christians to be equally confident or sanguine or light-hearted. Robert Leighton, a seventeenth century divine, of whom Coleridge said that he was the most inspired writer outside the canonical scriptures, said:

Some travel on in a covert, cloudy day, and and get home by it, having so much light as to

77

know their way, and yet do not at all clearly see the bright and full sunshine of assurance; others have it breaking forth at times, and anon under a cloud; and some have it more constantly. But as all meet in the end, so all agree in this in the beginning, that is, in the reality of the thing.

And lastly, this from a very different kind of man, James Anthony Froude, and this can be addressed to all of you:

It seems as if in a healthy order of things, to the willingness to believe there should be chained as its inseparable companion a jealousy of deception . . . Some men are humble and diffident, some are sceptical and inquiring; yet both are filling a place in the great intellectual economy; both contribute to make up the sum and proportion of qualities which are required to hold the balance even; and neither party is entitled to say to the other, "Stand by; I am holier than thou".

INTELLECTUAL OBJECTIONS

J. S. BEZZANT

ALL the objections discussed in these lectures, whether moral, historical or psychological, are intellectual in that they concern belief which is an intellectual activity. My assignment is with such as do not fall exclusively under others though related to them. As the lectures are addressed to persons in process of being educated [as the lecturers themselves are or should be] I do not phrase what I wish to say as I should do if I were speaking to, say, students of philosophy, nor shall I deal with specialist philosophical puzzles.

Few intellectual objections to Christianity are wholly or largely new. Some are its equal in age,

79

some older, though the latter are, of course, *re*directed against Christianity. Others are directed against what people think Christianity teaches, having gained their knowledge of it from ill-instructed Christians, but which are either not legitimate elements in it or not essential to it. I assume that religion, unless it is weaving a world of fancy into which to flee from the world of fact, must be integrated with other knowledge or probable beliefs about the world and man which are the proper concern of sciences and philosophy based upon them. These are far from having attained finality. Moreover they begin at the top of the intellectual scale and only gradually percolate to less learned people and, by the time they do so, are generally surpassed or out of date among scientists and thinkers at the top; whereas religion, if it is to have any great influence, must speak to all sorts and conditions of men and therefore the greater its influence the more it will be permeated by pre-scientific supposed knowledge and vague ideas, thus creating difficulties and objections as knowledge increases, or thought becomes more logical and precise. This is inevitable, and has always been so: it is intensified in an age in which knowledge of the world and man is rapidly increasing and has in many respects changed, as in our own age.

But objections, even if substantial, particularly in a time like the present, need not and are not likely to prove fatal: they may be seriously modified or overcome. Unless we are not to be sceptical of all positive statements while swallowing scepticism at one gulp with a credulity equalling that of biblical fundamentalists, objections against Christianity do not afford adequate ground for abandoning Christianity and dispensing with its practices or refusing to consider it more seriously. Such action or inaction is too much like easy religious dogmatism; and it is to cut oneself off from evidence far from irrelevant and to weight the scales negatively in advance. This is precisely what the prevailing secularism does, if I may use "secular" without the pejorative or bad sense which religious people commonly import into it. The disinclination to think about Christianity, the ignorance about it and the feeling that it is irrelevant are not very different from the closed minds of the narrower of biblical fundamentalists. But this prevailing attitude, at present presenting an insoluble difficulty for the churches, affords no basis for intellectual or other objections to Christianity; but even among the more thoughtful and influential objections are often grounded upon this prevailing attitude.

There is not, nor is there ever likely to be, any view of the meaning, purpose, value and destiny of human life, not even the view that it has none, that is not in a greater or less degree founded upon faith, for neither the negative nor the positive belief is demonstrable, i.e., capable of proof.

81

Judgment, whether positive or negative, to be worth consideration, depends upon whether the faith or the refusal of it, has actual and reasonable grounds. Nor, for this purpose, need we extend the meaning of faith beyond that which is very important for the continuation of some scientific researches. To cite but one instance—the efforts to find the cause or causes of cancer and its possible remedies. Conceivably these efforts may never be successful or the disease may cease to afflict mankind before they are. They have, so far, been baffled again and again, but the efforts to find them continue unabated: the sponge is not thrown in with anything like the ease with which difficulties in and objections to Christianity are allowed to be negatively effective.

Traditional Christianity has what was known as the scheme of salvation. It was based on Scripture regarded as the verbally inspired record of Divine revelation; and the scheme as a whole, but by no means all included in it, stands or falls with that view of the Bible. The Pauline teaching on sin and salvation was elaborated into a scheme containing elements of Aristotelian science and the theology of St Augustine. It began with an alleged rebellion of Satan against God in which angels fell. By direct acts of God, Adam and Eve were created, apparently as adults, not only innocent but fully righteous. Their descendants were intended to restore the number of the angels depleted by the heavenly revolt. Moved

82

by envy, Satan persuaded our first parents to disobey one absolute command of God, that they were not to obtain knowledge, and so brought about their fall from original righteousness, in consequence of which they transmitted to all their offspring, by natural generation, a corrupted nature wholly inclined to evil, an enfeebled will, and also the guilt of their sin. Thus all mankind lay under the curse of sin both original and actual, justly the object of Divine wrath and destined to damnation. In order to restore his thwarted purpose God sent his Son who, assuming human nature, was born on earth, whereon was wrought the drama of his death and resurrection. Jesus, pure from all defect of original and actual sin, alone fulfilled the conditions of a perfect sacrifice for human sin. By this God's legitimate anger with guilty mankind was appeased and his honour satisfied; he was graciously pleased to accept his Son's sacrifice, enabled to forgive sin, and man was potentially redeemed. The Christian church, a Divine corporation, came into being; those baptized into it who by grace persevered in the fulfilment of its commands would be secure in the life to come. From the supernatural life of the church, the world and history derived their meaning and without it would at a last day perish by fire. This would happen when the unknown number of souls required to replace the fallen angels was complete. The Anglican Prayer-book office for the burial of the dead still prays that God may be pleased shortly to accomplish the number of the elect and to hasten his kingdom. The dead would be raised from their graves in their bodies, despite St Paul's clear assertion that flesh and blood cannot inherit the kingdom of God nor corruption incorruption. The saved were predestined to their salvation by an inscrutable decree of God, not for any merits of their own, but solely for those of Christ. As to the fate of the rest, there were differences of opinion, but it was generally held that they would suffer endless torment in the flames of a hell, by which climax not only would God's power and justice be finally vindicated but heaven's bliss intensified.

This outline has been so shattered that the bare recital of it has the aspect of a malicious travesty. Known facts of astronomy, geology, biological evolution, anthropology, the comparative study of religions, race and genetical and analytic psychology, the literary and historical criticism of the Bible, with the teaching of Jesus and the moral conscience of mankind, have banished this scheme beyond the range of credibility. But though it can no longer be taken seriously, certain doctrines vital in the Christian gospel of salvation are still taught in forms which derive from the vanished scheme and from nothing else; and this hinders the effective presentation of Christianity today.

By far the most fruitful root of intellectual objections to Christianity is that, whatever view is taken of its origins, Christians could only interpret new facts and experiences in relation to the mythical world-pictures through which they apprehended them, whether Jewish or Hellenistic, both of which are irrelevant and impossible for our age and never again will be anything else. Inevitably the religious insights, so articulated and elaborated, appear almost equally irrelevant, a fact which present-day biblical theology so largely ignores and which deprives it of influence except among already convinced Christians. The primitive Christian preaching, now called the *kerygma* or proclamation, ante-dates the writing of anything in the New Testament. So far as it can be recovered it was a fragmentary outline, requiring much interpretative or explanatory comment to make it intelligible to converts. The inevitable results are clear enough in the New Testament. Jewish Christians found it hard if not impossible to transmute their inherited, largely mythopœic, ideas and so tended to circumscribe within them what was new and distinctive in the facts and message of Christianity, which was rejected by official Judaism and by those loyal to it. Hellenistic Christians (and Christianity's successes were and continued to be in the Graeco-Roman world —it has never widely or deeply influenced a Semitic civilization) tended to engulf the Christian message in a riotous speculation almost entirely lacking any historical or otherwise empirical or genuinely philosophical basis and which the modern world can only regard as little more than free imaginative composition. Then, when more serious thought undertook the exposition of Christianity and its rescue from this welter, it did so by large explanatory expansion of the apparent facts and theologizing upon them as recorded in the writings of the New Testament illumined, and as often darkened, by the Old, regarded as finally authoritative. But it did this on the basis of thought, often logical enough, but based upon thought-created entities, *a priori* ultimates, hypostatized abstract nouns treated as actualities, a procedure which issued, for good or ill, in results of centuries' duration, but which the modern world can only regard as pre-scientific philosophizing aloof from facts or as mythopœic fancy. Mercifully, in its œcumenical creed, the early Church confined itself almost exclusively to the words of Scripture; but the explanatory elaborations of theology have often counted for more in Christian life and thought than the reserved language of the creeds which consequently do not greatly help in dealing with contemporary objections.

Theologians today heavily over-emphasize the unity of the New Testament. What gives it such unity as it has is also fundamental in it—the supreme significance of the coming and of the person of Christ, about which there is neither difference nor controversy, though it is set forth in varying ideas, images or pictures. There is no integrated theological *system* in the New Testament. What it says about salvation through Christ is heavily coloured by Jewish apocalyptic-eschatological and Gnostic-like redemption mythologies. Biblical cosmology is mythical throughout, with its three-fold structure of the universe, the earth as the scene of Divine and subordinate angelic activity or of Satan and his daemons. Man cannot effectively control his own life for he may be possessed by evil spirits or God may inspire his thought and guide his purposes otherwise than by his reason. History likewise can be controlled by good and evil supernatural forces and does not follow a natural course. The existing æon or age is in bondage to Satan, sin and death; its end will come soon in a cosmic catastrophe preceded by terrible woes. The Judge will come from heaven, the dead will rise for final judgment and all men will be either saved or damned everlastingly. St Paul thinks God has sent a pre-existing Divine being, his son, who came to earth as a man; he dies the death of a sinner on the cross and so makes atonement for human sin. His resurrection is the beginning of the end, when death, the result of Adam's sin, shall be no more; daemonic spirits have already lost their power. Christ, risen and ascended to the right hand of God, will return to complete the redemption, human resurrection and judgment. St Paul, at one stage, thought he might be alive to witness it—"we shall not all sleep".

Meanwhile members of the church are united with Christ by faith, baptism and the eucharist, and can be sure of salvation unless they prove unworthy.

There can be no doubt that the demolition squad long ago did its work on all this. Bultmann, I think, greatly exaggerates the extent to which such mythology pervades the New Testament: there is much in it which bears no traces of its influence. But he can hardly exaggerate the intellectual objections which it generates in an age when the thinking of all who are widely influential is shaped by modern science, and by modern science rather than by philosophy. He is also right in saying that it is both senseless and impossible to accept either this mythical outlook or anything that depends upon it as being true. He knows, none better, that this is no new discovery and that all he says about it could have been said forty years ago. It was, and earlier. When I began the study of theology, what was called liberalism and, later, modernism, which had differing Catholic and Protestant forms, attempted to deal with the inescapable objections. Roman Catholic modernism was suppressed; liberal Protestantism attempted to free the Gospel from its mythology and to set it forth in thought forms of modern knowledge. The accommodations then made enjoy the benediction of malediction; they are now by general consent estimated to have been at least in part superficial

and not sustainable, though parts of them have
followed the well-worn course of being first
execrated, then derided as out of date and finally
claimed to have been always known and taught
by intelligent people. But the problems were and
remain genuine difficulties; and the subsequent
vogue of biblical theology, though it has brought
forth much fruit, leaves the basic problems and
objections unsolved, which is all a switching of
interest can do. It was partly motivated by fear
that liberalism eviscerated the Gospel. It has even
encouraged the resurrection of a biblical funda-
mentalism, regarded as stone dead in my youth,
and which biblical theologians themselves reject,
though I think they need and often subcon-
sciously assume something like it if they are to
commend to the modern world what, with an
extensive and sometimes strained selectiveness,
they put forward as the biblical view of the
world and man. For they seem to me to have no
satisfactory doctrine of Divine revelation distinguishable from what man, with mythical
outlooks, has made of it. Biblical theology cannot
set up limits to the scope and influence of human
thought based on knowledge, nor will its attempts
to do so ever again be widely accepted.

It is no part of the purpose of this lecture to
expound how Bultmann proposes to deal with the
modern challenge, but I think one aspect of it
adds to intellectual objections to Christianity. He
thinks it impossible to strip away the mythology

89

of the New Testament and retain the rest of it. The only course is to "demythologize" both the *kerygma* and its setting which he thinks can be done by a form of Existentialism which makes the New Testament speak to our human condition. But can it really be an answer to modern perplexities simply to *proclaim* that Jesus is manifested as the decisive saving event? It is even said that Christ crucified and risen meets us in the word of preaching and nowhere else. Faith in the word of preaching is sufficient and absolute. There is no possible philosophical natural theology, next to no reliable historical basis of Christianity. Believe the message and it has saving efficacy. But what is the ground for believing? The answer given is Jesus' disciples' experience of the resurrection. But this is not, he holds, a historical confirmation of the crucifixion as the decisive saving event because the resurrection is also a matter of faith only, *i.e.*, one act of faith has no other basis than another act of faith. And what is the resurrection? Another theologian who accepts the radical historical scepticism of Bultmann says "the resurrection is to be understood neither as outward nor inward, neither mystically nor as a supernatural phenomenon, nor as historical". If this has any meaning it can only be that the resurrection is not to be understood in any sense. No intelligent religious person desires to substitute prudent acceptance of the demonstrable for faith; but when I am told that it is precisely its immunity from proof which secures the Christian proclamation from the charge of being mythological, I reply that immunity from proof can "secure" nothing whatever except immunity from proof, and call nonsense by its name. Nor do I think anything like historical Christianity can be relieved of objections by making the validity of its assertions depend upon the therapeutic function it plays in healing fractures in the souls of believers, or understand how it can ever have this healing function unless it can be believed to be true.

It is less the facts of any science, many of which have no bearing whatever upon Christianity, from which objections arise, than by inferences from them. And it should never be forgotten that all sorts of inferences are much more commonly drawn from the *psychological impressiveness* of facts rather than from the careful reflection of reason upon them. Many years ago the late W. R. Inge wrote that the virtual disappearance of "the other world" from Christian preaching was the greatest change in it during his lifetime. An intellectual objection is the great improbability so widely felt about human immortality, which Christianity certainly teaches. I know the young are not much interested in this, naturally and rightly so. It would be unhealthy for those not far over the threshold of this life to be much concerned about another; nor can it be thought we are given life in this world to spend it wondering what happens when we leave it. Also the secular outlook of uneducated and unreflective people often makes them feel, when they hear the talk of life after death, that they are being put off their rights in this world by cheques drawn on the bank of heaven, the solvency of which they greatly doubt. But none of this removes the fundamental intellectual issue involved. So far as I know, if immortality were or should become demonstrable no established fact of science would require revision. The widespread objection is due to the psychological impressiveness of knowledge of what happens to embodied consciousness and all that depends upon it from anaesthetics or injuries to the brain, which can reduce a human person to a living block of material substances. How much more likely is it to be so when all the living physical processes we know cease at death? If to die is to become nothing, the intellectual objection to Christianity (though not to everything in it) is that the world cannot be regarded as realizing any *Divine* purpose.

Next, the doctrine of the Fall of man. It arose from human reflection which St Paul later once for all summarized, "the good which I would I do not: but the evil which I would not, that I practise". The Fall-doctrine purports to explain the *origin* of the manifest fact that man inclines to sin, does sin and is sinful. But it is objected that on the evolutionary view of man's origin and development, Adam and his transgression, or anything remotely resembling them, simply disappear from the data. And, as a matter of history, *Genesis* 3 was not the first story appealed to as explaining the fact of man's inclination to sin. Further, it is said, "fall" has no meaning except collapse or descent from higher to lower of which, except as moral evil or sin occurs in all men, history knows no trace; and apart from mechanical correctness or innocence (neither of which is either moral or immoral) righteousness, by the meaning of the word, cannot be created readymade, but must whether by effort or by grace or by both be attained. Moreover if the essence of sin is said to be man substituting his own desires, concern for himself, and his willing, for the will of God, it is an absurdity to say that primitive man was or could have been guilty of it; and if he did this when he became capable of doing so and that this sin of an unknown "Adam" corruptly affected all descendants, created a state of sin or in any degree explains why all sin, it is said that logical consequences follow which are as absurd as they are simple; for in as far as it necessitates these consequences, responsibility for the sin of all men is borne by the first sinner, while if there is any transmission of sin or of an inborn compulsive tendency to sin, we inherit the consequences of the sins of all our ancestors and the total burden would be borne by the last generation of mankind. The immense structure of doctrine, coupled with theories of atonement for sin, raised on *Romans* 5, 12–21 and other Pauline passages is often appalling to modern educated persons. Happily the great Christian oecumenical creed says nothing to justify these theories or the disputes they have engendered, and not even the Roman church is committed to the belief in the infallibility of St Paul.

The death of Jesus was the outcome of his absolute consecration of his life to his mission. His death was not his own act but that of the Jewish priests, the Roman procurator and his soldiers: to the end he himself seems to have been sufficiently uncertain as to its necessity to pray that if it were possible the cup might pass from him. There is also a curious *hiatus* in what St Paul says. He undoubtedly thought death was the consequence of sin and that the death of Jesus made possible the forgiveness of all sins. If he meant physical death, then that of Jesus manifestly delivers no one, even the redeemed, from death: if he means *spiritual* death it is impossible to begin to understand how the *physical* death of Christ can deliver man from that; it is simply unintelligible, not a profound mystery. Further, St Paul plainly thought that the death of Jesus was necessary but does not say why it was. Had he been pressed to do so I think (it is only a guess) he would have said "Because God had so willed" and might have supported that by an appeal to the Old Testament of a kind which would now have no relevance.

It is another objection that sinners are said to have suffered constructively the penalty of their sins when Christ bore it, because the humanity of the incarnate Divine suffered it. Some would say this involves an erroneous theory of punishment in that it supposes justice to require a penalty for sin independently of any moral or spiritual effect produced upon the sinner by it, but I do not wish to pursue that because if escaping consequences is a reason for seeking forgiveness it merely evinces that forgiveness has not yet touched a man, because its first result is to reconcile him to accepting the consequences and so to rise above them and the sins. But in the philosophical form of the theory the *a priori* Platonic doctrine of universals is mis-applied. A universal "humanity" is supposed to have an *actual* existence (as distinct from merely existing in the mind) so independent of its individual manifestations in human persons that "the universal" can be credited with the guilt of one of its particulars and can endure the punishment which all but one of the particulars do not endure, and yet to be so far inseparable from those manifestations that the endurance of the penalty can nevertheless be credited to each particular. Guilt, it is said, is corporate and implies a violation of the moral order for which humanity as a whole is responsible. The objection can be expressed thus: "It is clear we cannot have it both ways. If the universal is so real and independent that it can be punished without each

95

particular being punished, it cannot also be true that such a punishment endured by the universal can imply and involve its endurance by each and every particular: no juggling with universals will make it true to say that an individual who has in point of fact not been punished may nevertheless be deemed to have been punished. It is a logical fallacy to hold that everything which is true of one particular is true of each; while as to the theory that Christ is 'the universal of humanity' and not a particular man, that is surely a form of words to which no intelligible meaning can be attached. A particular man cannot also *be* a universal." If "the universal of humanity" meant only the *ideal* of humanity, it would be intelligible that Jesus was the ideal man; but then how the sufferings of an ideal man can benefit *unideal* men, except as they may tend to move them to penitence and amendment, would not be elucidated. If it be held that Jesus was not a particular man but a person in whom a universal or generic "humanity" was united with Divinity, such a theory, if it meant anything, would be inconsistent with the real humanity of Jesus in any intelligible sense; and that he was truly human is, perhaps, the one certain thing about him. On this matter an idealist philosopher such as the late Hastings Rashdall is in complete agreement with what any empirically based philosophy would maintain. And once it is acknowledged that we cannot be sure that we have the actual words of Jesus, one or two sayings attributed to him cannot weigh against his repeated teaching that God requires nothing but the penitence of the contrite heart to enable him to forgive, except that man must be forgiving towards other men who offend against himself.

From the modern point of view it is argued that moral evil (or, in a theistic context, sin) in beings of evolutionary development, is not a serious intellectual problem if man has a measure of freedom. An act of willing is morally evil if directed to an end which a man knows or believes is contrary to his duty; otherwise his act of willing, as such, cannot be intentionally morally evil, even if others judge it to be so. In a theistic context, his willing must also be opposed to what he thinks is the will of God. For the atheist, moral evil may be as real as anything that exists but it cannot properly be called sin, for there cannot be disobedience to a god who does not exist. I think that to all Christians, as to others, human life would lose both dignity and meaning if man had no measure of free choice. Is there, in human nature, as theology has often taught, and as the not unpopular neo-Calvinism appears to teach, only an ingrained bias to evil? If this is false or inadequate, as nearly all modern moral philosophers hold it to be and human practice certainly does, Fall-doctrine as an explanation of the fact that all do sin does not arise. It is said that the issue is not whether man's will is *often* evil but whether it

97

is *always* so. The answer of moral experience is not in doubt, and can be held to be more immediate and certain than any theories based on short passages in the writings of an apostle. There are innumerable acts of devotion to duty by multitudes of men and women as well as the most horrible cruelties and wickednesses. The sometimes almost incredible good is as real as the sometimes almost incredible evil. Desire and duty often conflict. Experience shows beyond doubt that man can rise to the one as well as fall to the other. If man were not tempted to do what he The desire itself is natural and there is no moral life. Desires arise out of what is morally neutral in that they can be turned to good or evil. The desire itself is rational and there is no evidence that it was ever anything else. A doctrine of inherent depravity, if it mitigated personal accountability, would mean that man's choices between good and evil are delusory. It is an induced delusion, not fact of experience, that man can of himself do no good thing. I think it would be hard to find anyone, whatever his religious beliefs, who would justify his own evil conduct by refusing responsibility for failure to resist temptation. Yet if, by his own effort, he cannot resist temptation, he has no responsibility for failure to resist it—a wholly demoralizing proposition. If, by his own effort, man cannot will or do what is not evil he cannot be justly blamed, either by man or God, if he does nothing but evil. There is no escape from this by saying that only by Divine grace can man will or do good; because, if God be creator and his nature includes love, to be totally outside the creator's enveloping grace is a condition in which no man can ever be except, perhaps, as he deliberately and consciously separates himself from it. If Divine grace is offered to man, not forced upon him against his will, man can accept or refuse it; and the choice between accepting or refusing grace is itself a choice between good and evil. If a man can choose to seek and respond to Divine grace, how can it be said he has no will to good? Only if God confers grace on some and not on others or if man's activity in accepting or refusing grace is comparable with the activity of a bucket when water is poured into it. The root of the doctrine of human depravity is not in direct experience but in the much more dubious statements of the Bible, reinforced by Augustine, regarded as revelation of propositional truth.

And here we contact a further objection, for modern theologians who are not Roman Catholics or biblical fundamentalists reject the notion of Divine revelation as consisting in the conveyance of propositional truths. Here also, it is widely felt, we reach the most fundamental and pervading objections to Christianity, for it is beyond doubt that Christian doctrine was elaborated on the basis of confidence that revelation was of this character—information, otherwise unattainable, imparted, if only fractionally, by the Deity. For the modern man, ever since biblical criticism emerged to produce confusion, science, philosophy and theology alike arose and have developed out of man's ineradicable urge to try to explain, when the knowledge requisite for explanation was scanty as compared with that now available. God cannot be regarded as revealing or inspiring notions destined to be found ethically and otherwise defective by man himself. Wherever morality has become decisive in man's theological opining, mythology has tended to become obsolete. The Old Testament itself is the classic example of the part played by ethical considerations in the advance and refinements of religious beliefs. But it is felt that this requires no belief in Divine revelation or inspiration *of a different kind* or source than is necessary to account for the Greek advances in philosophy and art, the Roman genius for law, or the amazing advances in the sciences in the modern world. "Nothing", it is said, "succeeds like success", specially if the first success be to have struck the road which leads to the goal. As for the supreme instance of revelation, the coming and teaching of Christ "in the fullness of time" it can be said that an Amos, Hosea, Micah, Isaiah and later Old Testament prophets would have been as capable as, if not more capable than, the majority of people today of understanding and appropriating the teachings of Christ had they been revealed to them. And

Divine revelation, whatever the Divine activity, implies the human reception and understanding of it for what it is. It is a fatal objection that there can be Divine revelation which is unassimilable by human understanding. Alleged revelation which is incomprehensible, whatever else it may be, is not *revelation*. There is an essential but easily concealed and overlooked implication in claiming that anything is true: it is that there are sufficient grounds for knowing or for reasonable belief that it is true. This is at once evident if we envisage the opposite statement, "This is true, but I have no grounds for knowing or believing it to be true", which is absurd. Human understanding and assimilation are involved in asserting the trueness of any proposition whatsoever.

What was said earlier about the philosophy of universals and particulars is also relevant to objections against the doctrines of the Incarnation and the Trinity, specially with reference to the incarnation as meaning that Christ was one person uniting two complete natures, the Divine and human. It is no valid objection to the idea of Divine incarnation that it cannot be fully explained in terms drawn from anything else; for if it be a fact, it is unique, and the unique cannot be wholly elucidated in terms drawn from anything else because, if it could be, that would abolish its uniqueness and reduce it to one instance of the otherwise common. But no knowledge, modern or other, does or can know or even envisage a complete human nature which is not also a human person. "Human nature" is nothing but an abstract noun connoting attributes which its use saves us from specifying at length. There is no ground or reason whatever, except baseless imagining, which justifies hypostatizing "human nature" into a "universal humanity" existing apart from its particulars. An "impersonal human nature" is as baseless as any idea can be. A human nature owes its characteristics *both* to the kind of body and to the kind of soul (if any) which constitutes a person; and the souls of men are, surely, not of the same order or kind as the creator of human souls. In any event, orthodoxy repudiated the notion that Christ had not a truly human soul. It can be said reasonably that the only theory which makes the idea of Divine incarnation intelligible is that the Divine in Christ functioned as a second subject, together with his human soul, of the experiences of Jesus. There is nothing inconceivable or contrary to knowledge in the thought that, in Christ, two subjects were combined in synthetic activities. Empirically based knowledge can afford no analogy; but how could it if the incarnation is unique? And this view seems to be required if the incarnation means, as it does, not the conversion of the Godhead into flesh but the taking of the manhood into God; for unless the resurrection and ascension are taken to mean the literal *absorption* of the manhood into God, which would involve the abolition of the manhood, the manhood must still function as one activity in the Divine being.

The same objection applies equally to the doctrine of the Trinity. The history of that doctrine shows nothing so clearly as that it is the attempt to think of an actual entity which can be described by the technical term "person" which is neither an individual person in the accepted meaning of the word nor an attribute or adjectival quality of a person, but something between the two, an entity which is neither noun nor adjective. As the human mind cannot conceive such an actuality it can reasonably be said that nothing can justify the assertion of its actual existence; and in spite of the difficulties, orthodoxy remains monotheistic and logical in asserting that God is one and therefore in being modalistic. The remaining objection is that then it does not enrich non-Trinitarian theism and that it seems to lose philosophic-theological importance. From the point of view of religious devotion the tri-unity of God is spoken of in language which renders it indistinguishable from tritheism; but that God is other than one is a departure, if an unconscious one, from orthodoxy.

It may be objected that Christianity over-personalizes the Divine. It would be much easier, in some respects, if we could think of God as concerned only with human life; but to do so is impossible and inconsistent with the conception of God as the creator or ground of the universe.

Creation, or absolute origination, is *ex hypothesi* ultimate, and therefore non-explicable: it would not be ultimate if it were. But no thoughtful person can ignore the fact that the universe, as modern astronomy reveals it, reveals no sign of *personal* activity. It may be psychological impressiveness, but none the less effective for being so, which leads men to think that the originator of inconceivably vast masses of flaming gas cannot be personal in any ordinary meaning of the word or that he or it can be in any sense specially concerned with one particular and relatively minute satellite of one small star among countless myriads and, at that, an elderly one which has long outgrown the turbulent heats of youth and is well on its way to join the more senile class of luminiferous bodies. I know that there are those who rejoice in what they call "the scandal of particularity"; but to the thoughtful mind it *is* the scandal in which they rejoice, a scandal which outrages thoughtful human minds. With one accord theologians acknowledge that we only speak of God as personal because that is the highest category of unity in diversity which we know. But having made their deferential bow to this inadequacy, they proceed to ignore it and continue to magnify the Lord in language which suggests that he is an inconceivably magnified personality, on the ground that all relations with him in religious experience are more like personal relationships than are our relations with things. I do not wish to be thought to maintain that religious experiences are an isolable source of knowledge. I think they are dependent upon beliefs and vary with beliefs; they can greatly enrich beliefs, but only if the beliefs are otherwise grounded. There is ample evidence that the effectiveness of beliefs of any kind depends, not upon their truth but on the intensity with which they are believed. Awe, veneration, worship, prayer, sacrifice, the sense of dependence, insignificance and guilt, instinctive obedience, need of purification, a sense of deliverance and joy— these are found in other living religions as in Christianity, and in cults which now have only historical interest. I think nothing but dogmatism can dismiss these activities and experiences of human nature as universal illusion. They may be regarded as the result of the "projection" of subjective cravings and wishes; and that may well be the *psychological* account of them. But it is a further question (and one which psychology which knows its limits and minds its own business and does not assume the disguise of science to masquerade as philosophy or theology will not attempt to answer) whether the projection is directed towards nothing or towards an invisible reality which evokes it. But it does not follow that religious experiences and activities point to a reality as their object, or that they entitle us to bestow a character and attributes upon that object, or to claim truth for a message proclaimed as his or its word without reference to other knowledge about the world and man, still less to ascribe to him or it a nature and attributes inconsistent with such other knowledge. Religious experience has found expression in various and inconsistent and even grotesque mythologies and theologies; and there may be other features of the universe which do not confirm the view of its nature or the kind of explanation of it which man's religious life indicates. It is only by reference to a wider range of experience and knowledge than purely religious experiences that reasonable men can find *grounds*, as well as *causes*, for religious beliefs that can claim truth. But as personality is the highest category we know which the world-ground has produced, the possibility of which must have been present in the primary collocations of the universe whatever they were, there is good ground for ascribing personality to its originator, provided we remember not to over-personalize the world-ground, or God. Whatever the difficulties of the doctrine of the Tri-unity of God, at least it enables us, as was said long ago, to speak of personality *in* God rather than of the personality *of* God. No one has or can have exhaustive knowledge of God as he is in himself. Human personality may be, indeed must be, but a faint copy of Divine personality. The essential in theism is that God, as the ground of the universe, must be an intelligent and ethical being. Thought of as apart from and prior to his world, God becomes a cosmologically useless idea. We can no more conceive a transition from a universeless God to God and a universe than logically move from an absolute one to a finite many. Any such attempts are nothing more than mythological imagining. We should conceive the Divine nature as including more than human personality immeasurably perfected, with capacities beyond our understanding as human knowledge transcends the cognition of an insect.

Intellectual objections to Christianity nowadays, in my judgment, and the fact that there are at present no convincing answers to them, both grow out of one root. This is that there is no general or widely accepted natural theology. I know that many theologians rejoice that it is so and seem to think that it leaves them free to commend Christianity as Divine revelation. They know not what they do. For if the immeasurably vast and mysterious creation reveals nothing of its originator or of his or its attributes and nature, there is no *ground* whatever for supposing that any events recorded in an ancient and partly mythopœic literature and deductions from it can do so. Nor is it anything but silly to pretend that the human mind cannot judge of such matters; for if it cannot, every ground for belief, unbelief or disbelief is taken away, because every propositional statement is the work of the human mind. It is also useless to proceed without investigation of the nature of what we call knowledge or beliefs based upon it, of how in fact we attain them; and the *basis* of such knowledge and beliefs must be empirical if it is to be anything other than baseless opining. This does not mean that anything incapable of empirical verification is either meaningless or untrue: it does mean that we can only proceed by analogy or symbolism, from what has an empirical foundation, to a natural theology, for we know ourselves and something about the creation before we know anything of God or gods, and there is nothing else by which to judge between competing and inconsistent claims that Christian or other religious doctrines rest on Divine revelation. Otherwise any claims that there has been such Divine revelation which can set limits to or override human thought is sheer dogmatism.

No one, I suppose, would regard the so-called "age of enlightenment", the eighteenth century, as other than almost unique in self-confidence, assurance of its own superior wisdom and its profound neglect of the accumulated experience of humanity; but it should have taught us one truth once and for all, namely, that though there must be many truths which any human mind does not know or of which it cannot perceive the truth, nothing can be true *for any mind* except as that mind can be brought to perceive its reasonableness as knowledge or belief, and that alleged revelation is of no use except as it enables man to attain his own insights. For "truth" is not a synonym for fact: it is the correspondence of mind with fact. For whatever God may reveal, human reception and understanding of it are involved in asserting it to be Divine revelation. Unintelligible or humanly unassimilable alleged revelation, whatever else it may be, is not *revelation*. If there be Divine revelation it may transcend but it cannot contradict what we have reasonable grounds for regarding as knowledge or reasonably grounded belief, because otherwise it implies an overriding of the proper dignity of the moral or ethical personality which God has created; and if He does *this*, God at the same time removes all possibility of human judgment as to whether it is Divine revelation or not.

The only possible basis for a reasonably grounded natural theology is what we call scientific. The difficulty is that there is no such actuality as "science"; there are many and increasing sciences. Their deliverances are not as yet mutually consistent. This is the root difficulty in constructing a natural theology. For myself, I cling to the hope that it will, in time, become possible. Meanwhile I think there is nothing that can be called knowledge or reasonable belief that there is or can be anything in the human mind that can possibly justify the passing of such a colossal condemnation on this inconceivably vast and mysterious universe as is implied in the judgment that it has no meaning or enduring value. Further, I think it is entirely reasonable for any man who studies the spirit of the facing of life as Christ faced it, and his recorded teaching, to decide that by him he will stand through life, death or eternity rather than join in a possible triumph of any evil over him. Whether or not any church will regard such a man as a Christian is nowadays wholly secondary and manifestly relatively unimportant: any church which refuses so to recognize him may be harming itself; it cannot harm him, and he should accept the refusal with regret but with equanimity.

This, I think, is the state of affairs in which, whether we like it or not, we do in fact live; and it will long continue. There is really nothing new in it. It took over 250 years for the church to reach a general agreement that Christ was fully Divine and fully human, well over another hundred years of debate about the relation of the Divine and human in him. Throughout this period the decisions of bishops in council and otherwise were bewildering in their contradictions and there was an insufferable strife of tongues which must have made it impossible for the ordinary man to know whether or no he was an "orthodox" Christian. But Christianity survived; and it will survive present difficulties, objections and uncertainties, though perhaps in a different form. Those who try to chart the Christian spiritual life of the intellectual saints distinguish in it a period which they call "the dark night of the soul" during which all the comforts and certitudes of the truth seem to be withdrawn. They have persisted and triumphed. This is the hard way and it is ours in this age. Christians sing in a saint's day hymn

> "They wrestled hard, as we do now,
> With sins, and doubts, and fears."

This is so often precisely what we do *not* do. We wish to make religion an escape from the conflict, a haven of refuge, and tend to enjoy the contempt for others which only a sense of religious superiority can give, forgetting that it is he who shall *endure* to the end who shall be saved.

THE AUTHORS

A. R. VIDLER is Dean of King's College and lectures in Ecclesiastical History.

D. M. MACKINNON of Corpus Christi College is the Norris-Hulse Professor of Divinity.

H. A. WILLIAMS is Dean and Tutor of Trinity College.

J. S. BEZZANT is Dean of St. John's College and lectures on the New Testament.